ACCUPLACER

Study Guide 2019-2020

PROUDLY PRINTED IN THE USA

ISBN

ACCUPLACER® is a registered trademark of College Board, which is neither affiliated with nor endorses this book.

Disclaimer: The ACCUPLACER exam may be updated and changed from time to time by the College Board. As such, the publisher takes all measures possible to ensure the highest of quality testing information, which means the information int his book may be replaced with new editions as exam standards evolve and change. Please note that the publisher accepts no liability should a customer purchase an older edition of any title that does not match the current standards of the ACCUPLACER exam.

ABOUT US

Advancements in technology have catapulted our ability to understand the workings of the human brain and how we learn and retain information. Cognitive and Nero-scientists understand better than ever that many things we've accepted as standards and best practices for decades are nothing of the sort…in fact, many of them are downright harmful to learning, typically leading to increased stress and less retained information.

So, why are all the study guides still the same as they were 20 years ago?

All study guides share one thing in common: they are a collection of a massive amount of information with no actual "guide" to it whatsoever. You buy their book and have to figure it out for yourself. Start on page 1 and hope for the best. We refused to accept that.

Combining seasoned educators who themselves challenged old standards, creative thinkers and professionals, and savvy entrepreneurs, we have shifted the paradigm.

With the book you hold in your hands now, every step is planned for you. Centered around a 30-day window, which is the average time test-takers start truly "studying" before the big exam, we are with you every step. Based on scientific study principles and cognitive research, you will increase information retention in fewer hours. In simple terms, you won't waste time, you'll reduce stress, and you'll be better prepared in the end.

No more cramming. No more guessing. No more stress.

CONTENTS

INTRODUCTION

As earlier mentioned, there have always been superstitions and generally accepted best-practices that no one bothers to question, or if they do, are considered an 'eccentric educator'. Here's some examples:

- Study somewhere quiet!
- Only focus on one subject at a time!
- Practice, practice, practice – memorize, memorize, memorize!
- The more you study, the higher your score!

Sound familiar? Those are so deeply ingrained in our way of thinking, that it boggles the mind to think otherwise. It seems common sense, but it's flat out wrong. Breakthrough discovery in recent years has shown time and again that our brains are wired to perceive and retain information in ways that are totally contrary to what we assumed were better.

Our study guides are based on 6 foundational principles:

1. Study multiple different sections in the same session.
On test day, you will have to switch gears multiple times in short succession. This is why it is so critical to study the way you will test, which is why we interleave subjects and concepts into each study session or module in this book. Your brain will be wired to quickly and efficiently switch gears as needed on test day.

2. Change your study environment frequently.

Your test environment will be totally different than your study environment, so get your brain used to it. Study in different locations, at a different time of day, and even listen to different music while you study. Our system schedules this for you to maximize achievement in each study session.

3. Do NOT over study.

Yes, over studying is certainly a thing. In fact, there is not only a point of diminishing returns for your time spent, but spending too much time studying can actually harm your score on test-day!

4. Take lots of breaks.

Take breaks. Take a lot of breaks in fact! Culturally, we have accepted the concept of "just pay attention" as though it is a choice we could make on purpose. The reality is lectures and lessons go far beyond the normal attention span for any person. This study guide has structured breaks timed for recharging your neurons and maximizing your study time.

5. Do NOT start studying too soon.

Again, more is not always better. Spending night after night for months on end will overwork your brain to the point you no longer actively retain information. Studying is about quality, not quantity: You don't get extra points on test day just for having spent more time with your nose in a book. This study guide is set up to maximize your time with short-bursts of studying, wherein you revisit concepts multiple separate times to reinforce your memory.

6. Self-testing is one of the best ways to learn.

Using practice tests to merely gauge your previous learning is only using a fraction of the intrinsic value of self-testing. In fact, self-testing is proven to be the most effective tool for learning! That is why we have 3 practice exams in this book, intended to be used at specific intervals to concretely solidify what you have previously studied.

CALENDAR

Day 1
Pre-Test

Day 2
Study
Module 1

Day 5
Review
Module 1

Day 6
Study
Module 2

Day 8
Review
Module 2

Day 9
Study
Module 3

Day 11
Review
Module 3

Day 12
Study
Module 4

Day 13
Review
Module 4

Day 15
Practice Test
1

Day 16
Targeted
Self-Study

Day 19
Review
Module 1
Self-Test

Day 20
Review
Module 2
Self-Test

Day 22
Review
Module 3
Self-Test

Day 23
Review
Module 4
Self-Test

Day 26
Targeted
Self-Study

Day 27
Targeted
Self-Study

Day 28
Review
Modules 1-4
Practice Test
2

Day 29
No Studying
Allowed -
Celebrate

Day 30
Take the
Test!

TARGETED SELF-STUDY
study your notes
and focus on your
weakest areas

SELF-TEST
flashcards
or a friend

CELEBRATE
reward yourself with a day off,
filled with your favorite activities
and foods!

EDUCATION IS LEARNING WHAT YOU DIDN'T EVEN KNOW YOU DIDN'T KNOW

FAQ

Q: Every time I try to make plans, something happens and I get off track. What if I cannot follow the schedule exactly?

A: Yes! Our system is designed around the fact that we all have lives, obligations, and other things to worry about than just studying. If you miss a day or have to cut a session short, just get back on track where you left off. No need to "make up for it", just pick right back up.

Q: I don't know if I trust this concept and like studying the old fashioned way...can I still use this book?

A: You sure can. This study guide still contains all of the information you need to pass your test, regardless of whether you follow the planned schedule or want to study your own way.

Q: What should I do during breaks?

A: First, be sure to take an actual break! Even if you feel like you don't need one, the break is for a reason beyond if you are feeling mentally fatigued.

Whatever you choose to do, do not even THINK about the material or the lessons. Preferably, do the most mindless thing you can. Hop on Facebook, look at cute cat videos on YouTube, go for a walk, fold some laundry...whatever you want as long as it's not mentally engaging!

Q: Oh no! I just got this book and my test is in a couple days! What do I do!?!?!

A: We've got good news! First, take a deep breath. While "studying" for long-term retention is the best, it is scientifically proven that "cramming" does actually work if you have no other option. You won't retain it for very long, but it will work! Even better news is this study guide is still better than any other option for cramming too. If this is your situation, get started now!

That's it! You understand the basics by now, and we don't want you to over-think it, because we've already done that for you! ust follow the calendar and the directions in the book.

First step: Take the pre-test. Yes, you read that right, friend. Don't even take a tiny peek at the lessons. Even if you are thinking "but I haven't looked at math problems in 10 years! I don't know where to start!" still take the pre-test first. In fact, the more remote the information seems to you now, the more you will benefit from the pre-test! We know it sounds crazy, but the science is sound.

About the ACCUPLACER

Congratulations! If you are reading this book, it means you have made the decision to continue your career, starting with the leap into higher education.

The first step of course is to max out your ACCUPLACER score. As you might know, the ACCUPLACER is what's called a "general aptitude exam" that helps colleges determine your baseline readiness and what courses you need to take.

You will be tested in reading, mathematics, and writing.

Scoring

Each school has its own standards and requirements which your admission counselor can help explain to you. However, there are some baselines you can count on which this book will help you prepare for.

Exam Breakdown

Below is the breakdown of the number of questions, and the type of questions, you will have to answer on the exam.

Section	Questions
READING	20
Information & Ideas	7-11
Rhetoric	7-11
Synthesis	2
Vocabulary	2-4
WRITING	25
Expression of Ideas	14-16
Standard English Conventions	9-11
MATHEMATICS	60
Arithmetic	20
Quantitative Reasoning, Algebra & Statistics	20
Advanced Algebra & Functions	20
Total	**105**

As you can see, not all test-takers will be given the exact same number of questions! Do not worry about this for now, the main focus is the concepts themselves.

PRE-TEST

As previously mentioned, this book has you take a "pre-test". If you feel like you are struggling and there are questions you don't understand…good! What that means is when you reach that lesson, your brain will remember "oh yeah! This is that one I couldn't figure out!". Your brain is automatically engaged and learning and retaining far better than if you hadn't struggled previously. What's even better? You'll remember it for longer too.

No cheating though! While it's OK, and even expected, that you will struggle and have to guess, it is critically important to try as hard as you can and especially important to not cheat and look up answers or clues. There is a proven science to this, you just have to trust it!

Here's a little secret you'll figure out later: The pre-test you're about to take is the exact same to Practice Test #1, and that's for a reason. First, you'll be able to truly gauge your increased performance, but it also will help reinforce the concepts and lessons you'll need for test-day.

Once you complete the pre-test, check your answers and make a note of it. Then, when you've completed the scheduled system of studying, you will take Practice Test #1 again and see how you improved.

Later, you'll take Practice Test #2 which has entirely new questions you won't have seen yet, so it will obviously be more challenging. Don't worry though! If you follow the system in this book, you'll be ready. In fact, most people are shocked at just how well they do.

With that…let's get started! Turn to the back of the book and find Practice Test #1.

MODULE 1

DAY, LOCATION, MUSIC

1 MONDAY, OCTOBER 12

COFFEE SHOP ON MAIN STREET

MY FAVORITE BAND

2

3

VOCABULARY

Expanding Your Vocabulary

The best, most natural way to expand your vocabulary is to read everything you can get your hands on. That means blogs, articles, social media, physical books, posted signs and even the labels on your shampoo bottle. Start looking for opportunities to read a little bit more every day, from now until the day of the test.

Of course, you do have that test coming up quick, so you don't have much time to go *au naturale.* We got your back. Here is your first and most crucial vocabulary hack: identifying root words.

What is the What?

Many words are little stories in and of themselves, which is to say that they have a beginning, middle and end. These parts are, respectively, the prefix, the root word and the suffix.

Not all words have all three parts. Sometimes it's just the prefix and root, sometimes just the root and suffix, and sometimes there are multiple roots. But—and this is important—a word is never just prefixes and suffixes. There is always at least one root word, because that's the main idea of the word. You can't have a complete, grammatically correct sentence without a subject, and you can't have a complete word without a root word.

For example, here's a word that's close to your heart lately: *reviewing.* It means viewing something again. Here are its parts:
Prefix = re
Root = view
Suffix = ing

Re is a prefix that means "again." *View* means "look." *Ing* is a suffix that denotes tense; it tells you the root word is happening in the present. So, if you're reviewing, you're currently viewing something again. The root word, or main idea of the word, is "view.

Let's get concrete: If you went up to one of your friends and just said, "Again," they would give you a funny look and say, "What again?"

It's the same idea if you went up to them and said, "Doing." They would say, "Doing what?"

If you went up to them and just said, "Look," they would get the point and try to see what you're seeing. They may not know what to look for, but they get the gist of what your trying to communicate to them. That gist is the root of the word.

Almost every vocabulary word on the test will be some combination of prefixes, roots and suffixes. If you run into one that you don't know, the first question to ask yourself is, "What is the what?"

Here is another example: *unemployment*
Prefix = un
Root = employ
Suffix = ment

You can't just say "un" or "ment" and expect to be understood, but when you add the main idea, *employ*, the word makes sense. It means the state of not having a job.

WHERE IT GETS MESSY

Of course, we speak the English language, which is a marvelous, madcap collage of many other languages, but mostly Latin, German and Greek. That means many root words are not English words. On top of that, there are no hard-and-fast rules for how prefixes and suffixes will change root words, so each root may look a little different depending on which prefixes and suffixes are used.

However, you can usually get the gist by breaking off the parts that you know are prefixes and suffixes and asking yourself what the remaining part reminds you of.

In order to break things down, you need to have a grasp of the most common prefixes, suffixes and root words you'll encounter on the test (these are outlined below).

COMMON ROOT WORDS
If you can't identify a word because it seems like it's in another language, that's most likely because it is. This isn't always true, but a good general rule is that our longer, more academic words tend to have their roots in Latin and Greek, while our shorter words tend to have their roots in German. For example, *amorous* and *loving* are synonyms, but one has its roots in the Latin *amor* and the other in the German *lieb*.

LATIN/GREEK - Because vocabulary words on the test tend toward the longer, more academic variety, you'll get the most out of studying some common Latin and Greek roots:

Root	Variations	What it Means	Examples
Aster	Astro	Star	Astronomy, disaster
Aqua		Water	Aquatic, aquarium
Aud		Hear	Auditorium, audience
Bene		Good	Benevolent, benign
Bio		Life	Biology, autobiography
Cent		Hundred	Century, cent (money)
Chrono		Time	Chronological, synchronize
Circum	Circa	Around	Circumspect, circumnavigate
Contra	Counter	Against or conflict	Contraband, encounter
Dict		Speak or say	Dictate, dictation
Duc	Duct, duce	Lead or leader	Produce, conduct
Fac		Make or do	Manufacture, facsimile (fax)
Fract	Frag	Break	Fraction, defragment
Gen		Birth or create	Genetics, generate
Graph		Write	Telegraph, calligraphy
Ject		Throw	Inject, projection
Jur	Jus	Law	Juror, justice
Log	Logue	Concept or thought	Logo, dialogue
Mal		Bad	Maladaptive, malevolent
Man		Hand	Manuscript, manual
Mater		Mother	Maternal, material
Mis	Mit	Send	Mission, submit
Pater	Pat	Father	Paternal, patriot
Path		Feel	Sympathy, empathetic
Phile	Philo	Love	Philosophy, anglophile
Phon		Sound	Telephone, phonetic
Photo		Light	Photograph, photosynthesis
Port		Carry	Transport, portable
Psych	Psycho	Soul or spirit	Psychiatrist, psyche
Qui	Quit	Quiet or rest	Acquittal, tranquility
Rupt		Break	Rupture, interrupt
Scope		See, inspect	Telescope, microscopic
Scrib	Script	Write	Describe, transcription
Sens	Sent	Feel	Sensory, consent
Spect		Look	Spectate, circumspect
Struct		Build	Construct, obstruction
Techno	Tech	Art or science	Technical, technology
Tele		Far	Teleport, television
Therm		Heat	Thermometer, thermal
Vac		Empty	Vacation, evacuate
Vis	Vid	See	Visual, video
Voc		Speak or call	Vocal, vocation

PREFIXES - Here are your opposite prefixes, which you'll encounter a lot on the test:

Prefix	Variations	What it Means	Examples
Anti-	Ant-	Against or opposite	Anti-inflammatory, antagonist
De-		Opposite	Decontaminate, deconstruct
Dis-		Not or opposite	Disagree, dis (slang for insult)
In-	Im-, Il-, Ir-	Not	Incapable, impossible, illegitimate, irreplaceable
Non-		Not	Noncompliant, nonsense
Un-		Not	Unfair, unjust

Here is a quick list of some other common prefixes:

Prefix	Variations	What it Means	Examples
En-	Em-	Cause	Enlighten, empower
Fore-		Before	Foresee, foretell
In-		Inside of	Inland, income
Inter-		Between	Interrupt, interaction
Mid-		In the middle of	Midair, midlife
Mis-		Wrong	Mistake, misdiagnose
Pre-		Before	Pregame, prefix
Re-		Again	Review, recompress
Semi-		Half or partial	Semitruck, semiannual
Sub-		Under	Subconcious, subpar
Super-		Above	Superimpose, superstar
Trans-		Across	Translate, transform

SUFFIXES - Here are some common suffixes you'll encounter on the test:

Suffix	Variations	What it Means	Examples
-Able	-Ible	Can be accomplished	Capable, possible
-Al	-Ial	Has traits of	Additional, beneficial
-En		Made of	Molten, wooden
-Er		More than	Luckier, richer
-Er	-Or	Agent that does	Mover, actor
-Est		Most	Largest, happiest
-Ic		Has traits of	Acidic, dynamic
-Ing		Continues to do	Reviewing, happening
-Ion	-Tion, -Ation, -Ition	Process of	Occasion, motion, rotation, condition
-Ity		The state of	Ability, simplicity
-Ly		Has traits of	Friendly, kindly
-Ment		Process/state of	Enlightenment, establishment
-Ness		State of	Happiness, easiness
-Ous	-Eous, -Ious	Has traits of	Porous, gaseous, conscious
-Y		Has traits of	Artsy, fartsy

Vocabulary Practice Test

For items 1-5, try to identify the root and write an English translation or synonym for it. We did the first one for you as an example.

#	Word	Root	Translation/Synonym
Ex	Description	Script	Something written
1	Irresponsible		
2	Entombment		
3	Professorial		
4	Unconscionable		
5	Gainfully		

For items 6-10, identify the prefix and write an English translation or synonym for it.

#	Word	Prefix	Translation/Synonym
Ex	Prepare	Pre	Before
6	Proceed		
7	Misapprehend		
8	Antibiotic		
9	Hyperactive		
10	Cacophony		

For items 11-15, identify the suffix and write an English translation or synonym for it.

#	Word	Suffix	Translation/Synonym
Ex	Lovable	Able	Can be accomplished
11	Tedious		
12	Absolution		
13	Cathartic		
14	Merriment		
15	Inspector		

Now, it's time to test your current vocabulary:

16. Achromatic most nearly means:
a. full of color
b. fragrant
c. without color
d. vivid

17. Cursory most nearly means:
a. meticulous; careful
b. undetailed; rapid
c. thorough
d. expletive

18. Hearsay most nearly means:
a. blasphemy
b. secondhand information that can't be proven
c. evidence that can be confirmed
d. testimony

19. Magnanimous most nearly means:
a. suspicious
b. uncontested
c. forgiving; not petty
d. stingy; cheap

20. Terrestrial most nearly means:
a. of the earth
b. cosmic
c. otherworldly/unearthly
d. supernatural

ANSWER KEY

1. response

2. tomb

3. profess

4. conscience

5. gain

6. pro-

7. mis-

8. anti-

9. hyper-

10. caco-

11. -ious

12. -tion

13. -tic

14. -ment

15. -tor

16. (c) without color

17. (b) undetailed; rapid

18. (b) secondhand information that can't be proven

19. (c) forgiving; not petty

20. (a) of the earth

CRITICAL READING

FINDING THE MAIN IDEA

Many of the reading comprehension questions you will encounter on the exam are structured around finding the main idea of a paragraph. The last section on root words was all about finding the main idea of a word – notice a theme developing here?

In this section, you will need to find the main idea of a paragraph. Luckily, that's nice and simple once you know what to look for.

First of all, we're going to re-define a few terms you might think you already know, so don't rush through this part:

PARAGRAPH

A paragraph is a tool for organizing information. It's simply a container for sentences in the same way that a sentence is a container for words. Okay, maybe you knew that already, but you'd be surprised how many

professional writers get their minds blown when they realize that almost all books are structured in the same way:

Books are made of...
Chapters, which are made of...
Sections, which are made of...
Paragraphs, which are made of...
Sentences, which are made of...
Words

It's a simple hierarchy, and smack in the center is the humble paragraph. For the purposes of the test, you need to be able to comb through given paragraphs to find two kinds of sentences: topic and detail.

TOPIC SENTENCE

A well-written paragraph, which is to say all of the paragraphs that you'll find on the test, contains just one topic. You'll find this in the topic sentence, which is the backbone of the paragraph. The topic sentence tells you what the paragraph is about. All of the other sentences exist solely to support this topic sentence which, more often than not, is the first or last sentence in the paragraph. However, that's not always the case, so use this foolproof method: Ask yourself, "Who or what is this paragraph about?" Then find the sentence that answers your question.

Detail Sentence

Detail sentences exist to support the topic sentence. They do so with all kinds of additional information, such as descriptions, arguments and nuances. An author includes detail sentences to explain why they're writing about the topic in the first place. That is, the detail sentences contain the author's point, which you'll need in order to find the main idea. To easily spot the author's point, just ask yourself, "Why is the author writing about this topic?" Then pay close attention to the detail sentences to pry out their motivations.

Got it? Good. Now, let's do some really easy math: The topic + the author's point = the main idea.

Now, let's put that in English:
What + Why = Main Idea

In the Real World

All right, you've got the abstract concepts nailed down. Now, let's get concrete. Imagine a scenario where a friend is explaining the movie *Toy Story* to you. Also, imagine that she has already picked her jaw up off the floor, because seriously, how have you not seen *Toy Story*? You should fix that.

She tells you what the movie is about: There are these toys that get lost, and they have a bunch of adventures trying to get back to their owner. Then she tells you why you should see it: It's cute and funny, and it's a classic.

Two sentences: The topic (what the movie is about) and the author's point (why she's telling you about it.) And now you have the main idea: Your friend thinks you should see the movie Toy Story because it's a cute, funny classic about toys having adventures.

Illustrating the Main Idea

Here is a paragraph similar to one you might encounter on the test, followed by the types of questions that you will need to answer:

Example 1 – from *The Art of Conversation* by Catherine Blyth:

"Silence is meaningful. You may imagine that silence says nothing. In fact, in any spoken communication, it plays a repertoire of roles. Just as, mathematically speaking, Earth should be called Sea, since most of the planet is covered in it, so conversation might be renamed silence, as it comprises 40 to 50 percent of an average utterance, excluding pauses for others to talk and the enveloping silence of those paying attention (or not, as the case may be.)"

This one is relatively easy, but let's break it down:

Who/What is the paragraph about? Silence.

Why is the author writing about this topic? It is often overlooked, but it's an important part of conversation.

What is the main idea? Silence is an important part of conversation. Or, put it another way: "Silence is meaningful" - it's the first sentence!

Okay, you've seen the technique in action, so now it's your turn. Read the following paragraphs and determine the topic sentence, the author's main point, and the main idea.

Example 2 – from *Love, Poverty and War* by Christopher Hitchens

"Concerning love, I had best be brief and say that when I read Bertrand Russell on this matter as an adolescent, and understood him to write with perfect gravity that a moment of such emotion was worth the whole of the rest of life, I devoutly hoped that this would be true in my own case. And so it has proved, and so to that extent I can regard the death that I otherwise rather resent as laughable and impotent."

1. The main topic of this paragraph is:
a. gravity

b. adolescence

c. death

d. love

2. The author's main point about this topic is that:

a. it is something to be resented

b. it is something to laugh at

c. it makes life worth living

d. it is brief

3. The final sentence is:

a. the topic sentence

b. the author's main point

c. detail sentence

d. the beginning of a new topic

4. The main idea of the paragraph is that:

a. a moment of love is worth all of life's woes

b. adolescence is something to laugh at

c. Bertrand Russell is very wise

d. death is something to be resented

EXAMPLE 3 – FROM *RIVER OF DOUBT* BY CANDICE MILLARD

"Theodore Roosevelt, one of the most popular presidents in his nation's history, had vowed never to run again after winning his second term in the White House in 1904. But now, just eight years later, he was not only running for a third term, he was, to the horror and outrage of his old Republican backers, running as a third-party candidate against Democrats and Republicans alike."

5. The topic of this paragraph is:

a. Teddy Roosevelt

b. early 20th century politics

c. independent presidential candidates

d. the election of 1912

6. Why does the author mention "old Republican backers?"

a. Roosevelt's backers were all elderly

b. Roosevelt used to be a Republican

c. Roosevelt used to be a Democrat

d. they backed Roosevelt eight years ago

7. Where is the topic sentence?

a. the last sentence

b. the first sentence

c. it is likely stated before the chosen selection

d. it is likely stated after the chosen selection

8. The main idea of the paragraph is:

a. Roosevelt was a popular president

b. Roosevelt ran for a third term as a third-party candidate

c. early 20th century politics had three parties

d. the election of 1912 had three candidates

EXAMPLE 4 – FROM *LOVE IN THE TIME OF CHOLERA* BY GABRIEL GARCÍA MÁRQUEZ

"To him she seemed so beautiful, so seductive, so different from ordinary people, that he could not understand why no one was as disturbed as he by the clicking of her heels on the paving stones, why no one else's heart was wild with the breeze stirred by the sighs of her veils, why everyone did not go mad with the movements of her braid, the flight of her hands, the gold of her laughter. He had not missed a single one of her gestures, not one of the indications of her character, but he did not dare approach her for fear of destroying the spell."

9. The main topic of this paragraph is:

a. a beautiful woman

b. fear

c. love

d. seduction

10. The author uses many details to:

a. show that the man is obsessive

b. show the vividness and intensity of love

c. make people admire his writing ability

d. show that the woman is unique

11. The topic sentence:

a. is the final sentence

b. is the initial sentence

c. also contains many details

d. is not present in this paragraph

12. The main idea of the paragraph is that:
a. the man is afraid of the woman he loves
b. the woman doesn't even know the man is alive
c. love is vivid and intense
d. there is no main idea because this is fiction

EXAMPLE 5 – FROM *ON LOOKING* BY ALEXANDRA HOROWITZ

"Part of human development is learning to notice less than we are able to. The world is awash in details of color, form, and sound – but to function, we have to ignore some of it. The world still holds these details. Children sense the world at a different granularity, attending to parts of the visual world we gloss over; to sounds we have dismissed as irrelevant. What is indiscernible to us is plain to them."

13. The main topic of this paragraph is:
a. what humans notice or don't
b. human development
c. the world's details
d. children

14. The author's main point about the topic is that:
a. children see more details than adults
b. adults see more details than children
c. aging inevitably results in wisdom
d. the world is very complicated

15. The first sentence is:
a. the topic sentence
b. the author's point
c. a detail sentence
d. the beginning of a new topic

16. The main idea of the paragraph is:
a. children and adults live in different worlds
b. as you age, your experience of the world gets richer
c. what is indiscernible to children is plain to adults
d. as you age, you notice less than children do

ANSWER KEY

1. d	9. a
2. c	10. c
3. b	11. b
4. a	12. c
5. c	13. a
6. a	14. a
7. d	15. b
8. a	16. a

BREAK TIME (15 MINS)

PERFORM AN ENJOYABLE ACTIVITY TO DISTRACT
YOU FROM STUDYING.
READ SOMETHING LIGHT, GO FOR A WALK —
WHATEVER YOU DO, TRY TO GET
YOUR MIND OFF THE MATERIAL
FOR A LITTLE WHILE.

ARITHMETIC BASICS

Before you begin studying for the arithmetic section of the exam, let's talk basics. Many math exams will test your memory of basic math definitions, vocabulary, and formulas that have become so distant that the questions on this type of exam may feel unfair. You likely don't refer to quotients and integers in your day-to-day life, so testing your recall of high school math class vocabulary and concepts doesn't exactly feel like a valid way to gauge your mathematical reasoning abilities. Well, as the French say, "C'est la vie!" or "That's life!" Perhaps the most appropriate English expression would be, "You gotta do what you gotta do."

In this section, it's best for you to begin with a refresher list so that you can master basic math terminology quickly.

INTEGER: Any whole number, i.e. any number that doesn't include a non-zero fraction or decimal. Negative whole numbers, positive whole numbers, and 0 are all integers. 3.1415 is not an integer. ½ is not an integer. -47, -12, 0, 15, and 1,415,000 are all integers.

POSITIVE AND NEGATIVE NUMBERS: A positive number is any number greater than zero. A negative number is any number less than zero. Zero is neither positive nor negative. Adding a negative number is the same as subtracting the positive value of that number. Subtracting a negative number is the same as adding a positive number.

EVEN AND ODD NUMBERS: An even number is any number that can be evenly divided by 2, with no remainder left over. -4, 2, 6, 24, and 114 are all even numbers. An odd number has a remainder of 1 when it is divided by 2. -19, 1, 3, 5, 17, and 451 are all odd numbers. Another way to think about even/odd is that even numbers are all integers that are multiples of two, and odd numbers are any integers that are not multiples of two.

FACTORS AND MULTIPLES: The factors of a number (or a polynomial) are all of the numbers that can be multiplied together to get the first number. For example, the following pairs of numbers can be multiplied to get 16: 1 * 16, 2 * 8 and 4 * 4. Therefore, the factors of 16 are 1, 2, 4, 8, and 16. Note: a polynomial is an expression that can have constants, variables and exponents, and that can be combined using addition, subtraction, multiplication and division.

PRIME NUMBER: An integer that only has two factors: 1 and itself. There are two things to remember: (1) out of all of the infinite integers in existence, there is only one prime number that is even, and that is the number 2 — that's it, and (2) you can handle almost any prime number question on the test by memorizing all of the primes between 0 and 100. This is not required, but you will save time and mental anguish if you do this. Here they are:

2, 3, 5, 7, 11, 13, 17, 19, 23, 29, 31, 37, 41, 43, 47, 53, 59, 61, 67, 71, 73, 79, 83, 87, 89

PRIME FACTORIZATION: The prime numbers you have to multiply to get a number. Take the number 24. First, you should find the factors of 24: 1, 2, 3, 4, 6, 8, and 12. Then, you need to pull out all the numbers that are not prime: 1, 4, 6, 8, and 12. What's left? 2 and 3 are the prime factors of 24! Now, that's a simple example, but the concept remains the same, no matter how large the number. When in doubt, start working from the number 2 (the smallest prime), which will be a factor of any number that ends with an even number. Be on the lookout for sneaky questions. For example, if the exam asks you for the prime factors of the number 31, for instance, recall that 31 is a prime number (but 1 is not!) so the only prime factor it can possibly have is itself — 31. The same goes for all prime numbers.

SUM: Add — the number you get when you add one number to another number.

DIFFERENCE: Subtract — the number you get when you subtract one number from another number.

PRODUCT: Multiply — the number you get when you multiply one number by another number.

QUOTIENT: Divide — the number you get when you divide one number by another number.

EXPRESSIONS

An expression is made up of terms that are numbers, variables, and operators which are added together. If that sounds complicated, expressions are simply made up of the basic symbols used to create everything from first-grade addition problems to formulas and equations used in calculus. The individual terms of the expression are added to each other as individual parts of the expression. Remember that expressions may stand for single numbers, and use basic operators like * and ÷. However, a single expression does not suggest a comparison (or equivalency). But an equation does and can be represented by a simple expression equal to a number. For example, $3 + 2 = 1 + 4$ is an equation, because it uses the equal sign. So, think of $3 + 2$ and $1 + 4$ as building blocks — they are the expressions that, when joined together by an equal sign, make up an equation. Another way to think of an expression is that it is essentially a math metaphor used to represent another number.

ORDER OF OPERATIONS

An operation is what a symbol does. The operation of a + sign, for instance, is to add. That's easy enough, but what happens if you run into a problem like this?

$$44 - (3^2 * 2 + 6) = ?$$

You have to solve this equation by simplifying it, but if you do it in the wrong order, you will get the wrong answer. This is an incredibly important concept. This is where the Order of Operations comes in — here's what you have to remember.

1. Parentheses
2. Exponents

3. Multiplication and division (from left to right)
4. Addition and subtraction (from left to right)

You must do these operations in order, starting with parentheses first and addition/subtraction last, in order to get the correct answer.

$$44 - (3^2 * 2 + 6) = ?$$

Start by focusing on the expression in parentheses first. Inside the parentheses, you will find an exponent, so do that first so that you can do the operation within the parentheses:

$$3^2 = 3 * 3 = 9$$

then the expression becomes $(9 * 2 + 6)$

To complete the operation within the paragraph, you need to remember to do the multiplication operation first:

$$9 * 2 = 18$$

$$(18 + 6) = 24$$

You don't need the parentheses anymore because there are no operations left to complete inside of them. Now the problem looks like this:

$$44 - 24 = ?$$

$$20 = ?$$

You can use the phrase, Please Excuse My Dear Aunt Sally as a useful mnemonic. It has the same first letters as parentheses, exponents, multiplication, division, addition, subtraction.

However, the most common mistake involving the order of operations is the following: doing division after multiplication and subtraction after addition, which results in the wrong answer. You have to do multiplication and division as you encounter it from left to right, and the same goes for addition and subtraction. Remember to do what is inside parentheses first, and that might require you to do exponents, multiplication/division, and addition/subtraction first.

Here's another example of this concept:

$$(4^2 + 5^3 - 120) * 3 = ?$$

$$4^2 = 4 * 4 = 16$$

$$5^3 = 5 * 5 * 5 = 125$$

PLEASE
EXCUSE
MY
DEAR
AUNT
SALLY

PARENTHESES
EXPONENTS
MULTIPLICATION
DIVISION
ADDITION
SUBTRACTION

$$(16 + 125 - 120) * 3 = ?$$

$$21 * 3 = ?$$

$$63 = ?$$

If you didn't understand this example, you should go back and review the Order of Operations again.

Occasionally, you may encounter an equation that uses brackets. You should think of brackets as super parentheses, i.e. it's at the top of the list, and so you do that first, before anything else.

EQUATIONS

Equations relate expressions to one another with an equal sign. In algebra, they can get pretty complicated, but in arithmetic, equations often center around finding the equivalent of a single expression. For instance,

$$3 + 2 = 5$$

It may seem pretty simple to say $3 + 2$ expresses 5 because they have a clear and simple relationship — they are equal. Other kinds of equations, i.e.

relationships, include symbols like > (greater than) and < (lesser than), which can join two expressions together. These are often called inequalities since they are not equal. The greater than or less than relation is a sign of inequality.

Remember that equations can be rearranged by doing the same operations to each side of the equivalency. Here's an example of subtracting 6 from both sides of the equation:

$$34 - 23 = 6 + ?$$

$$34 - 23 - 6 = 6 + ? - 6$$

The number 6 subtracted on both sides of the equation cancel each other out. The equality of the relation remains unaffected.

$$11 - 6 = ?$$

$$5 = ?$$

GREATEST COMMON FACTOR

Sometimes the term Greatest Common Factor is called the Greatest Common Divisor, but either way, the concept is the same - it's the largest factor that two (or more) numbers share.

To use this concept, you should first work out all of the factors for each number and then find the largest factor they have in common. For example, find the Greatest Common Factor of 18 and 30:

The factors of 18 are: 1, 2, 3, 6, 9 and 18
The factors of 30 are: 1, 2, 3, 5, 6, 10, 15 and 30

The highest number in both sets, i.e. the highest number that are common to both sets, is 6, so that's your Greatest Common Factor.

LEAST COMMON MULTIPLE

Sometimes the term Least Common Multiple is called the Lowest Common Multiple or the Smallest Common Multiple or the Lowest Common Denominator when used in a fraction, but in any case, the concept is the same - without knowing this term, you can't compare, add, or subtract fractions, and that's important.

The least common multiple is the smallest number that can be divided by two (or more) given numbers. To get this number, first write out the multiples for each number and then find the smallest multiple that they share.

For example, find the Least Common Multiple of 3 and 7:

The multiples of 3 are: 3, 6, 9, 12, 15, 18, 21, 24, 27...
The multiples of 7 are: 7, 14, 21, 28, 35, 42, 49, 56...

The lowest number in both sets is 21, so that's your Least Common Multiple. Notice that there are other multiples, but we are interested in the lowest or least of the common multiples.

EXPONENTS AND ROOTS

EXPONENTS

An exponent is an algebraic operation that tells you to multiply a number by itself.

For example, 4^2 is the same as $4 * 4$, and 4^3 is the same as $4 * 4 * 4$. The exponent tells you how many times to multiply the number by itself.

Exponents have a few special properties (you can think of them as shortcuts or even helpful tricks if you want):

1. If two numbers with exponents share the same base number, you can multiply them by adding the exponents:

$$2^5 * 2^3 = 2^8$$

2. If two numbers with exponents share the same base number, you can divide them by subtracting the exponents:

$$2^5 \div 2^3 = 2^2$$

3. A number with an exponent raised to a negative power is the same as 1 over or the reciprocal of that number with an exponent raised to the positive power:

$$5^{-2} = 1/5^2$$

$$1/5^2 = 1/25 \text{ or } 1 \div 25 = 0.04$$

4. A number raised to a fraction power is the same as a root, or radical:

$9^{1/2} = 3$ (the square root indicated by the two in one half)   Remember that the root of a number x is another number, which when multiplied by itself a given number of times, equals x. For example the second root of 9 is 3, because 3 * 3 = 9. The second root is usually called the square root. The third root is usually called the cube root. Because 2 * 2 * 2 = 8, 2 is the cube root of 8. Two special exponent properties are explained more in the two examples below.

1. 1 raised to any power is 1; for example:

$$1^2 = 1$$
$$1^{-4} = 1$$
$$1^{912} = 1$$

2. Any number raised to the power of 0 equals 1 — sounds crazy, but it's true! Here's an example:

$$253^0 = 1$$

If you can remember these six properties, you'll be able to simplify almost any problem with exponents.

Roots and Radicals

Roots and radicals are sometimes held up as cliché symbols for difficult math problems, but in the real world, they're easy to understand and use to solve equations.

A radical is an expression that has a square root, cube root, etc; the symbol is a $\sqrt{}$. The number under that radical sign is called a radicand.

A square is an expression (not an equation!) in which a number is multiplied by itself. It is often said that the given number is raised to the power of 2. Here's an example: 4^2 is a square. 4 * 4 is the same square, expressed differently.

The square root of a number is a second number that, when multiplied by itself, will equal the first number.

Therefore, it's the same as squaring a number, but in the opposite direction. For example, if you want to find the square root of 25, we have to figure out what number, when squared, equals 25. With enough experience, you will automatically know many of the common square roots. For example, it is commonly known that 5 is the square root of 25. Square and square root are operations that are often used to undo or cancel out each other in problem-solving situations. A mental image, kind of like a numerical mnemonic, that helps some people is to think of the given number and the square root (in the above case, 25 and 5) as the tree and its much smaller roots in the ground.

The previous example uses the number 25, which is an example of a perfect square. Only some numbers are perfect squares – those that are equal to the product of two integers. Here's a table of the first 10 perfect squares.

It is helpful to remember that if you find that the square root of any radicand is a whole number (not a fraction or a decimal), that means the given number is a perfect square.

To deal with radicals that are not perfect, you need to rewrite them as radical factors and simplify until you get one factor that's a perfect square. This process is sometimes called extracting or taking out the square root. This process would be used for the following number:

$$\sqrt{18}$$

First, it's necessary to notice that 18 has within it the perfect square 9.
$$18 = 9 * 2 = 3^2 * 2$$

Therefore, $\sqrt{18}$ is not in its simplest form. Now, you need to extract the square root of 9

$$\sqrt{18} = \sqrt{9} * 2 = 3\sqrt{2}$$

Now the radicand no longer has any perfect square factors.

$\sqrt{2}$ is an irrational number that is equal to approximately 1.414. Therefore, the approximate answer is the following:

$$\sqrt{18} = 3 * 1.414 = \text{approximately } 4.242$$

Note that the answer can only be an approximate one since $\sqrt{2}$ is an irrational number, which is any real number that cannot be expressed as a ratio of integers. Irrational numbers cannot be represented as terminating or repeating decimals.

Factors	Perfect Square
1 x 1	1
2 x 2	4
3 x 3	9
4 x 4	16
5 x 5	25
6 x 6	36
7 x 7	49
8 x 8	64
9 x 9	81
10 x 10	100

FACTORIALS

If you have ever seen a number followed by an exclamation point, it's not yelling at you – it's called a factorial. Simply put, a factorial is the product of a number and all of the positive integers below it, stopping at 1. For example, if you see 5!, its value is determined by doing the following example:

$$5! = 5 * 4 * 3 * 2 * 1 = 120$$

Factorials are typically used in relation to the fundamental principle of counting or for the combinations or permutations of sets.

ALGEBRA CONCEPTS

Algebra is a branch of Mathematics with symbols, referred to as variables, and numbers, as well as a system of rules for the manipulation of these. Solving higher-order word problems is a valuable application of the Algebra properties described in this chapter.

EXPRESSIONS

Algebra uses variables, numbers and operations as the basic parts. Variables are typically represented by letters and may have any number of values in a problem. Usually the variable is the unknown quantity in a problem. All letters can and often are used, but x, y, and z are letters that appear most often in algebra textbooks. In a testing situation, letters other than x, y, and z are often used to mislead test takers. Algebraic expressions are variables and numbers with operations such as addition, subtraction, multiplication

and division. The following are all examples of algebraic expressions:

x	y	a	(letters)
7u	$1/2$ q (or $q/2$)	3.9 p	(product of a variable and number)
s + 5	u+v	2.3+r	(sum of a variable and number)
z − 3.5	k-n	t − 1.3	(difference of a variable and number)
m/6	$(z/2)$	3.9 /p	(quotient of a variable and number)
c^2	$b^{0.5}$	$\sqrt{3}$	(variable or number with an exponent)

Finally, the sum, difference, product or quotient of these items are also expressions.

EQUATIONS

Equations are defined as algebraic expressions that are set equal to a number, variable or another expression. The simplest identifier of an equation is the equal sign (=). When an equation is written to express a condition or represent a situation for problem solving, the solution is normally completed by manipulating the equation correctly so that a variable or unknown quantity is on one side of the equal sign and the numerical answer(s) are on the other side of the equal sign. Let's review some problem-solving methods in the following examples.

If the simple equation is written in word form, the first step must be to write the equation that represents that written question. The simple problem of ages of individuals is a common example:

Example 1: Jane is 8 years older than Nancy. In 5 years, she will be 27 years old. What is Jane's age now?

The variable J will represent Jane's age and the expression J+5 will represent Jane's age in 5 years. In this example, we read that this expression is equal to a number, in this case 27. Our equation becomes:

$$J+5 = 27$$

In the words of the problem, we have the correct expression set equal to a number. Our basic principle is to perform algebraic operations until the "J" is alone on one side of the equation and the numerical answer is on the other side. This type of solution involves the opposite of the addition (+5) so 5 is subtracted from both sides.

$$
\begin{array}{r}
J+5 = 27 \\
-5 \quad -5 \\
\hline
J+0 = 22
\end{array}
$$

Therefore, the answer says that the variable J, Jane's age, is now 22 years.

If the simple equation involved multiplication, the steps would involve an opposite operation that in this case would be division.

$$7J = 84$$
$$7J/7 = 84/7$$
$$J = 12$$

These examples are typical of "one-step solutions" since a single operation is involved to solve the problem.

Of course, there are multiple step solutions in more involved problems. But the rules are still the same, i.e.

1. Opposite operations are performed to solve
2. The same operations must be performed on both sides of the equation
3. The solution is complete when a variable is on one side and the answers are on the other side

Example 2: Jane is 8 years older than Nancy. In 5 years, she will be twice as old as Nancy. What is Jane's age now?

The first step to solving this type of problem is to identify the variable. In this solution, we will select the variable "J" to represent Jane's age and "N" to represent Nancy's age.

The two equations from the word description, become:

$$J - 8 = N$$

and

$$J + 5 = 2(N+5)$$

Dividing both sides of the second equation by 2 means that it becomes

$$(J+5)/2 = N+5$$

Adding 5 to the original equation we have

$$J - 8 + 5 = N + 5$$

In this method, there are two expressions which contain "J" that are both equal to "N + 5" so therefore, they must be equal to each other. So:

$$J - 3 = (J + 5)/2$$

Multiply both sides by 2 (same operation on both sides) and the equation is:

$$2J - 6 = J + 5$$

Subtract J and add 6 to both sides and the answer becomes:

$$2J - 6 = J + 5$$
$$-J + 6 \quad -J + 6$$
$$J = 11$$

By this solution, the problem is completed and the following statements are clarified:

1. Now, Jane is 11 years old, and Nancy is 3 years old.
2. In 5 years, Jane will be 16 years old, and Nancy will be 8 years old.

We are able to answer the question, "What is Jane's age now?" and all the other ages in the question because of an algebra principle that requires two equations for two unknowns. In the problem, there are two variables (J and N) and two relationships between them (now and 5 years from now). If we are able to formulate two equations with the two unknowns, then algebra principles will allow for the solution of a complex problem.

QUADRATIC EQUATIONS

Quadratic equations are algebraic equations where the largest variable exponent is equal to two. This is often referred to as a "second degree" equation. If there are multiple terms, it can also be referred to as a second degree polynomial, where polynomial indicates that there are multiple terms in the equation. Quadratic equations are valuable in higher-order problem solving situations, with particularly important application in Physics problem solving. Examples are

depicted below:

$$7x^2 = 0$$

$$\frac{1}{2} (9.8) \, t^2 = 27$$

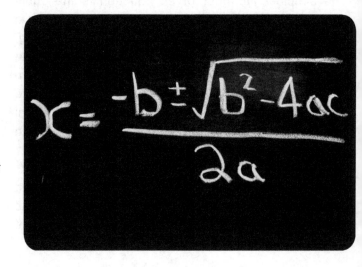

$$ax^2 + bx + c = 0 \text{ where a, b and c are real numbers}$$

Note that all quadratic equations can be written in the form of the last example because coefficients can be zero and algebra operations can be performed so that the 0 is on the right side of the equation. This last statement is the standard form and is of great importance. Every quadratic equation in this form can be solved with the quadratic formula. It is presented here with a qualifying statement. In a timed testing environment, the use of the following formula is typically used when factoring is not feasible, since it is a time consuming option.

The quadratic formula for equations in the standard form states:

$$x = \frac{- b +/- \sqrt{(b^2 - 4ac)}}{(2a)}$$

Due to the complexity of the quadratic formula, it will normally be used when the term

$$(b^2 - 4ac) / (2a) = 0$$

$$(b^2 - 4ac) / (2a) = \text{a perfect square}$$

Since the use of technology is not allowed, any more intricate application of the quadratic formula will be too time consuming to be useful. Note that the operations before the square root sign are both correct. The plus and minus signs indicate that every quadratic equation has the possibility of two answers. It does not say that both answers will be valid to the multiple-choice word problem that is in quadratic form. This is easily explained with a simple statement. Since two negative numbers and two positive numbers multiplied together give a positive answer, any quadratic equation may have two possible correct answers. When answering questions about quadratic equations in multiple-choice problems, that statement should be considered.

FOIL – POLYNOMIAL MULTIPLICATION

Polynomial multiplication is routinely taught with a method described as FOIL, which stands for First, Outside, Inside and Last. In a binomial multiplication problem, the form will usually look like this, with A, B, C, D whole number coefficients:

$$(Ax + B) * (Cx + D)$$

- The "First" means that Ax and Cx are multiplied together to equal ACx^2
- The "Outside" means that Ax and D are multiplied together to equal ADx
- The "Inside" means that B and Cx are multiplied together to equal BCx
- The "Last" means that B and D are multiplied together to equal BD

    The polynomial answer becomes:
    $ACx^2 + (AD + BC)x + BD$

In testing conditions, this method can be cumbersome, confusing and unreliable because mistakes are too common.

A simplified alternative is called the Box Method, and it is simpler for multiple reasons.

1. There is a box that provides the organization for the multiplication.

2. The box also provides organization for the addition of like terms.
3. This method is expandable for use with longer polynomial multiplication.

To use the Box Method for polynomial multiplication, follow these steps:

1. Create a box that has a row and column for each term in the multiplication problem.
2. Perform the multiplication of each pair of terms.
3. Place the answers in the cells of the box.
4. Add the like terms that are aligned diagonally.
5. Write the polynomial.

The following diagram explains the outcome with the previously noted example:

$$(Ax + B) * (Cx + D) \text{ becomes:}$$

The diagonal boxes in the upper right and lower left are always the "like terms" so there are no questions as to which terms must be added. This is true if you have ordered the binomials correctly with the "x term" of the binomials on the left and on top, respectively.

The final outcome is the same as the FOIL answer previously noted:

$$ACx^2 + (AD + BC)x + BD$$

Notice also that the Box Method has the additional benefit of separating the addition and multiplication operations completely.

In a multiple-choice problem such as this, there is a significant benefit in using the box method as a time saving technique.

Example: $(x + 6)(4x + 8) = $ (choose a correct answer below)

(A) $4x^2 + 32x + 48$
B $4x^2 + 32x + 32$
C $4x^2 + 32x + 14$
D $4x^2 + 14x + 48$

$4x^2 + 8x + 24 + 48x$

$4x^2 + 16x + 24$

$4x^2 + 8x + 24x + 48$

$4x^2 + 32x + 48$

The lower right box entry means that the last term in the answer must be 6 * 8, or 48. So, both answers B and C can be eliminated because the last term is not 48.

	Ax	B
Cx	ACx²	BCx
D	ADx	BD

The upper right and lower left box entries are added and the middle term must be 24x + 8x = 32x. So, answer D can be eliminated because the middle term is not 14x.

The correct answer must be A, a choice that can be made logically by looking at the box entries. Eliminating choices is expedited with the Box Method because the box entries can be easily compared to coefficients in the answer choices.

SUBSTITUTE VARIABLES

Many mathematics applications involve using equations and then substituting variables. This terminology means that the algebra equation will typically have a single variable with all other parameters defined as whole, decimal or fractional numbers. Then to solve a specific problem, the value of the specific variable will be uniquely defined (in some cases, multiple values may be supplied for comparison) and the variables used to determine a problem solution. For example, let's use the equation that was previously discussed, for a car traveling 70 miles per hour:

Distance traveled equals 70 mph multiplied by time in hours

Without the words, in strictly algebraic terms:

$$D = 70t \text{ (t in hours)}$$

To find the amount of distance traveled, solve the equation by substituting the value of time that is

appropriate for the problem. If the problem stated that the time traveled was two and one-half hours, then the equation would be solved with the following:

$$D = 70 * 2.5$$

After multiplying, the answer for the distance traveled is 175 miles.

In some equations, you may be asked to evaluate an equation that involves a second-degree variable. For example, a word description might read as follows:

Distance traveled is equal to one-half 9.8 m/sec² multiplied by the time squared

Again, without words, in strictly algebraic terms the equation would be:

$$D = \frac{1}{2} * 9.8 * t^2$$

Evaluating this equation for a time of 2 seconds becomes:

$$D = \frac{1}{2} * 9.8 * 2^2 = \frac{1}{2} * 9.8 * 4 = 2 * 9.8 = 19.6 \text{ meters}$$

The answers have distance units that are determined by the units of measure that are given in the word problem.

Miles per hour multiplied by hours will provide distances in hours. Meters per second per second will provide distances in meters. The units of time and distance within the problem must be consistent. Substituting variables will be simple if the variables are consistent.

INEQUALITIES – GREATER THAN AND LESS THAN

Inequalities are an algebra topic that is often misrepresented and taught in a more difficult manner than necessary. When we find solutions to algebra equations there is a single number (or two numbers in the case of a quadratic equation) that represents the set of all numbers that are equal to the algebraic expression on the other side of the equal sign.

Inequalities represent the set of all numbers that are either greater than or less than that specific solution. If the number 3 represents the solution of an algebra equation, then the number line diagram above may help visualize what the inequalities may look like:

The arrow on the left side of the "o" is the less than inequality, and the arrow on the right side of the "o" is the greater than inequality. Of course, the "o" represents the exact solution of the inequality. This simplicity tells us that the simplest way to solve the inequality is to first solve the equality and then find out which arrow is required. The solution with quadratics will be discussed at the end of this section.

The inequality $7x + 2 > -5$ will be solved by first solving the equality:

$$7x + 2 = -5$$

Following the steps discussed in section 2, the first step is to subtract 2 from both sides and divide both sides by 7. The solution of the equality says:

$$x = -1$$

To see which way the arrow points, we will use the value of $x = 0$ in the inequality to see if it is true. If it is true, then the arrow pointing to the right is correct (>), which is what we would expect. If $x = 0$ is not true then the arrow must point the other direction (<). The test helps by ensuring that the point at $x = 0$ is or is not in the solution set of the inequality, allowing the correct answer to be chosen.

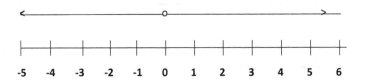

Therefore, substituting $x = 0$ means:

$$7(0) + 2 = 2$$

Since 2 is greater than negative 5, the answer looks like the following diagram:

The arrow does not include the point "0" on the number line because the "Zero Test" tells us that that point does not satisfy the inequality. If the "0" is not included then the arrow must point to the left of the point at -1, which was the answer to the equality. If our test showed that the "0" satisfied the equality, then the arrow would have pointed to the right. For this reason, both "Greater Than" and "Less Than" are addressed in this section. They are determined the same way, specifically:

First, find the solution to the equality.

Second, test to see if $x = 0$ is true for the inequality.

If the test is true, the solution must include the point $x = 0$.

If the test is not true, the inequality goes the opposite direction.

There may be the question as to why the value of $x = 0$ is chosen for the test. Simply, it represents the simplest solution for evaluating algebra equations with variables. Any term which has an "x" (or x^2 or higher order) simply disappears when $x = 0$, leaving only the constant numerical terms.

If there is a need to solve an inequality where the equality solution is $x = 0$, then the inequality test can be performed with $x = 1$. The test is almost as simple as the zero test, and it applies if the equality solution is 0. The same logical decision process used for the zero test also applies here.

MODULE 2

DAY, LOCATION, MUSIC

1
MONDAY, OCTOBER 12

COFFEE SHOP ON MAIN STREET

MY FAVORITE BAND

2

3

VOCABULARY

Words in Context

When reading through a chapter in a book or a passage on a test, you will sometimes encounter a word you've never seen before. You may not know what it means, but don't worry! You can still figure out a basic definition of the word, even if you don't have a dictionary in hand (or if you don't want to get off the sofa and get one).

In every sentence, any given word is surrounded by clauses, phrases and other words. When you find a word you don't recognize, you can learn more about it by studying the context surrounding it. These surrounding words, phrases and clauses are called context clues. Using these, you can determine the definition for almost every unfamiliar word you encounter. This is a skill that will become especially helpful when you start reading higher-level texts with fancy words or training manuals with lots of jargon.

Types of Context Clues

As you read, you can use several different types of context clues to help you discover the meaning of unknown words. Some important and common types of context clues are outlined below. Try to use the specific context clue to determine the meaning of the bolded word.

Root Word & Affix

This is a context clue that uses your existing knowledge of common root words.

EXAMPLE: Scientists who dig up dinosaur bones are experts in **PALEONTOLOGY.**

This context clue assumes you have knowledge of dinosaurs and can relate that to the study of "paleontology."

COMPARE/CONTRAST

This is a context clue that signals a similarity or difference by using words or phrases that denote a comparison or contrast. Words that imply similarity (or comparison) include *like*, *also*, *just as*, *too*, etc. Words that imply difference (or contrast) include *whereas*, *opposed to*, *unlike*, *versus*, etc.

EXAMPLE: A COMET, LIKE AN **ASTEROID**, IS MADE FROM LEFTOVER MATTER IN THE UNIVERSE.

This context clue compares an "asteroid" with a comet to imply a similarity to the given definition of a comet.

LOGIC

This is a context clue wherein you must infer the definition of the unknown word by using the relationships within the sentence.

EXAMPLE: BUILDERS ROUTINELY USE **FASTENERS** THAT WILL HELP HOLD THEIR STRUCTURES AND BUILDINGS IN PLACE.
This context clue describes the job that "fasteners" do.

DEFINITION

This is a context clue that includes a basic definition of the unknown word.

EXAMPLE: NEW BIOLOGICAL SPECIES CAN BE FORMED THROUGH A PROCESS CALLED **SPECIATION**.
This context clue defines "speciation" outright.

EXAMPLE OR ILLUSTRATION

This is a context clue that uses an example or illustration of the unknown word.

EXAMPLE: ANIMALS CLASSIFIED IN THE PHYLUM PORIFERA LIVE IN A **MARINE** HABITAT LIKE THE ATLANTIC AND PACIFIC OCEANS.

This context clue uses Atlantic and Pacific Oceans as examples of "marine" habitats.

HOMOGRAPHS

Now that you've had a refresher on context clues, let's talk about homographs. A homograph is a word that is spelled exactly like another word, but has a different meaning. For example, "bass" can mean "a low, deep sound" or "a type of fish." Here's a more complex homograph: "minute" can mean "a unit of time" or "something very small."

Although questions with homographs aren't necessarily difficult, you'll need to pay extra attention to the context clues. If you're rushing or don't read the entire sentence, you can accidentally mark an incorrect answer by mistaking the homograph for the wrong meaning. As long as you take your time and use the context clues, you'll most likely have no problem.

Here's something to consider when you take the exam. Within the question, replace the vocabulary term with your selected answer choice. Read the sentence and check whether or not it makes sense. This won't guarantee a correct answer, but it will help identify an incorrect one.

Another point to keep in mind is that sometimes there will not be an answer choice that exactly fits into the sentence. Don't panic! You probably did not misread the context clues or come up with an incorrect meaning. Many times, questions will ask you to select the *best* word from the given answer choices, even though that correct answer choice may not be the best *possible* answer overall. These types of questions want you to choose the *most* correct answer choice. These can be tricky to tackle, but expect to see questions like this on the exam. Just remember the

CRITICAL READING

DETAIL QUESTIONS

Reading passages and identifying important details is an important part of the critical reading process. Detail questions ask the reader to recall specific information about the main idea. These details are often found in the examples given in the passage and can contain anecdotes, data or descriptions, among other details. For example, if you are reading a passage about certain types of dogs, you may be asked to remember details about breeds, sizes and coat color and patterns. As you read through the passage, make sure you take note of numbers, figures and the details given about the topic. Chances are you will need to remember some of these.

There is a wealth of information, facts, pieces of data and several details that can be presented within any passage you read. The key to uncovering the main idea and understanding the details presented is to take your time and read through everything contained in the passage. Consider each example and figure presented. Think about how they relate to the main idea, how they support the focus, and how those details add to the information and value of the passage.

Strategies for Answering Detail Questions:

- Identify key words in the question that help you find details and examples to answer the question.

- Take note of how words are used and if phrases are repeated. Look for the overall meaning of each paragraph and passage.

- Some questions will pull words or phrases from the passage and quote them in the question. In this case, find those quotes and make sure they are being used the same way in the passage and the question. Many questions will change the meaning of these to make the question wrong or confuse the reader.

- Some questions will ask you to determine if a particular statement or topic is true. In this case, look over the paragraphs and find the overall theme or idea of the passage. Compare your theme or idea to the statement in the question.

UNDERSTANDING QUESTION STEMS

In addition to careful reading of the passages (including marking up the text for topic and concluding sentences, transitional words and key terms), you must also be able to identify what is being asked of you in each of the questions. Recognition of the task in each question can be easily accomplished if you are familiar with the question stems, or the most commonly phrased wording that will be associated with each type of question on the test. Keep reading for an explanation of each question type, along with sample stems, and suggested approaches for tackling them.

Supporting Details

Supporting details are those that back up the main ideas presented in the passage. These can include examples, clarifying explanations, or elaborations of basic ideas presented earlier in the reading. Supporting details are directly stated in the passage, so you must rely on your careful reading to guide you to the correct answer. Answers may not be stated in the original language of the passage, but the basic ideas will be the same. Here are some common ways this type of question is asked:

· The passage states...
· The author says...
· According to what you read...

Main Idea

Questions asking you to identify the main idea expect that you will be able to determine the overall point of the passage (often called the thesis), NOT secondary details or supporting points. Attempting to put the main idea into your own words after reading WITHOUT looking at the text again is a very helpful strategy in answering this type of question. If you can sum up the author's main point in your own words, then you will find it very easy to find the right "match" amongst the answers provided for you. Alternately, the main idea may often be found in the opening or concluding paragraphs, two common places where an author may introduce a topic and his perspective about said topic, or he summarize the main points. Here are some common ways this type of question is asked:

· The main idea for this paragraph...
· The central point of the passage...
· A possible title for the passage...
· The author's primary point...

Inference

Inferences are those ideas which can be gleaned from the suggestions that may be implied in other statements made by the author. They are never explicitly stated, but we understand that they are true from "reading between the lines". The answers to inferences questions, therefore, are assumptions, and cannot be found from direct statements in the text. You will have to rely on your ability to logically deduce conclusions from your careful reading. More than one answer may sound correct, but only one is. Make sure that, whichever answer you choose, you can find statements in the text which would support that idea. If you cannot do that, then that choice is likely not the right answer. Here are some common ways this type of question is asked:

· The passage implies...
· The author suggests... ·
  The reader could logically conclude that...
· The reader would be correct in assuming that...

Tone/Attitude

Some questions will ask you about the author's tone or attitude. A good place to start with this type of question is to consider whether the passage is positive, negative or neutral. Does the author seem angry? Maybe sad? Or torn between two points of view? The language that an author uses can be very telling about his tone and attitude. Is the author critical? Praiseworthy? Disappointed? Even if you find some finer details of passage difficult to understand, the tone and attitude are often fairly easy to identify. Look for adjectives and statements that reveal the author's opinion, rather than facts, and this will help you know his tone or attitude. Here are some common ways this type of question is asked:

· The tone of the passage is...
· The attitude of the author is...
· The writer's overall feeling...

Style

Style refers to a writer's "way with words". Most seasoned writers have a well-developed and easily recognizable style, but often the topic of a written work can dictate style. If the topic is serious the language will likely be more formal. Works for academic settings may be heavy with the jargon of that discipline. Personal reflections can be rife with imagery, while instructional manuals will use simple and straightforward language. Identifying style is not difficult; simply pay attention to the words used (simple or fancy?), the sentence structure (simple or compound-complex?), as well as the overall structure of the piece (stream of consciousness or 5-paragraph essay?). You must answer these questions in order to determine the style of the passage. Here are some common ways this type of question is asked:

· The overall writing style used in the passage...
· The author's style is...
· The organizational style of the passage is...

Pattern of Organization

Pattern of organization questions want you to consider how the writing of a piece was developed. What features did the writer utilize to make his point? Did he include personal anecdotes? Data or statistics? Quotes from authorities on the topic? These are all modes of organizing a passage that help the writer support his claims and provide a logical focus for the work. Here are some common ways this type of question is asked:

· The author proves a point through...
· In the passage, the author uses...
· Throughout the passage, the author seems to rely on...

Purpose and Attitude

Questions asking about purpose and attitude require you to consider why the author took the time to write. The authors motivations are directly behind the purpose of the piece. What question did he wish to answer? What cause did he want to show support for? What action did he wish to persuade you to take? Identifying these reasons for writing will reveal the purpose and attitude of the passage. Here are some common ways this type of question is asked:

· The purpose of the passage is...
· The author's intent for writing the passage is...
· The attitude the author displays is...

Fact/Opinion

There will be some questions on the test that will ask you whether a statement is a fact or an opinion. Without being able to fact-check, how will you do this? A rule of thumb would be that opinions reflect only the thoughts, feelings or ideas of the writer, whereas facts are verifiable as true or false, regardless of one's feelings. If a writer cites a statistic about the environmental effects of oil drilling on migratory mammals in the Pacific Northwest, then that is verifiable and can be considered factual. If, however, the writer claims that oil drilling in the Pacific Northwest United States is bad and should be stopped, then that is his opinion. He may at some point provide examples of why this is so, but that viewpoint is based on his thoughts and feelings about oil drilling, and can only be considered opinion. Here are some common ways this type of question is asked:

· Which statement is a fact rather than an opinion?
· This statement is meant to be...
· An example of fact is when the author says...
· An example of opinion is when the author states that...

ELIMINATING WRONG ANSWERS

An author often writes with an intended purpose in mind, and they will support their main idea with examples, facts, data and stories that help the overall meaning of their written text to be clear. You may be asked a question regarding one of these details or examples, or you may be asked something about the overall theme or main idea of the passage. These types of questions require you to read the passage carefully for meaning and to look at all the supporting details used. However it's also important to learn how to identify incorrect answer choices and eliminate them right away. This will help you narrow down the answer choices that are likely to be correct.

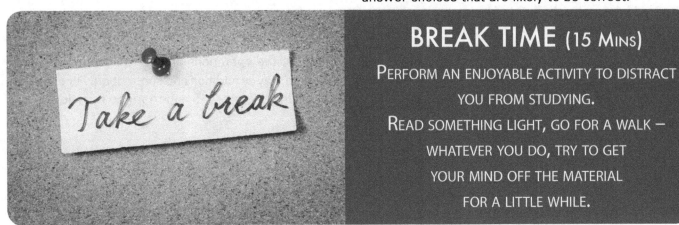

Take a break

BREAK TIME (15 MINS)

PERFORM AN ENJOYABLE ACTIVITY TO DISTRACT YOU FROM STUDYING.
READ SOMETHING LIGHT, GO FOR A WALK — WHATEVER YOU DO, TRY TO GET YOUR MIND OFF THE MATERIAL FOR A LITTLE WHILE.

ARITHMETIC REASONING

ADDITION, SUBTRACTION, MULTIPLICATION, DIVISION OPERATIONS WITH DECIMALS

The sign conventions for positive and negative decimal arithmetic operations are the same as those for whole number operations outlined in Module 1. But, there are special details to recall when performing arithmetic operations with decimal values to ensure correct answers.

When adding and subtracting decimal values, it is important to make sure that the decimal points are aligned vertically. This is the simplest method to ensure a reliable result. For example adding 0.522 and 0.035 should be performed as follows:

```
  0.522
+0.035
───────
  0.557
```

Subtraction operations should be aligned similarly.

```
  0.522
−0.035
───────
  0.487
```

It is important to note that multiplication requires a different convention to be followed. When multiplying decimals, the operations are NOT aligned necessarily the same way as addition and subtraction. For example, multiplying 0.7 and 2.15 is performed as follows:

$$\begin{array}{r} 2.15 \\ \times\ 0.7 \\ \hline 1.505 \end{array}$$

When multiplying decimal values, the decimal point placement in the answer is determined by counting the total number of digits to the right of the decimal point in the multiplied numbers. This detail is often overlooked in testing choices where the same numbers may appear in several multiple-choice answers, but with different decimal point placements.

Division of decimal values is simplified by first visualizing fractions that are equivalent. The mathematics terminology is that a dividend / divisor = quotient. For example:

7.35 / 1.05 is the same as 73.5 / 10.5, which is the same operation as 735 / 105.

The last fraction, in the example above, means that to solve 7.35 / 1.05 we can divide 735 / 105 and find the correct whole number answer. This method just requires that when dividing by a decimal number, the divisor must be corrected to be a whole number. This requirement is achieved by moving the decimal points in both the dividend and divisor the same number of decimal places. If the dividend still contains a decimal point, the place is maintained in the long division operation, and the correct quotient is still achieved. The quotient remains in the form of a decimal number.

ADDITION, SUBTRACTION, MULTIPLICATION, DIVISION OPERATIONS WITH FRACTIONS

The sign conventions for positive and negative fractional arithmetic operations are the same as those for whole number operations outlined in Module 1. However, there are special details to recall when performing arithmetic operations with fractional values to ensure correct answers.

Remember that fractions are made up of a numerator and a denominator. The top number of the fraction, called the numerator, tells how many of the fractional parts are being represented. The bottom number, called the denominator, tells how many equal parts the whole is divided into. For this reason, fractions with different denominators cannot be added together because different denominators are as different as "apples and oranges." So, when adding or subtracting fractions with different denominators, a common denominator must be found. In this case, simple geometric models will be used to explain the common denominator principle. Usually, this principle is illustrated with circles divided into "pie slices." A simpler and more effective example involves the use of squares or rectangles divided into fractional parts.

Representing fraction parts, $\frac{1}{3}$ and $\frac{1}{4}$ will be demonstrated with the following square diagrams. In this case a whole square is the number "1" and the fractional parts will be the slices of the square as follows:

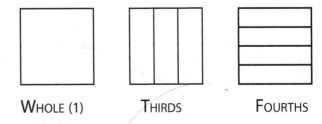

WHOLE (1)   THIRDS   FOURTHS

If we superimpose the four horizontal slices over the three vertical slices, there are twelve separate parts of the whole as follows:

In the last diagram, any column representing a third, has four of the twelve small rectangles from the diagram, or $\frac{4}{12}$ as the equivalent fraction. Similarly, any row of the last diagram, representing a fourth, has three of the twelve small rectangles from the diagram, or $\frac{3}{12}$ as the equivalent fraction. With this modification of the two fractions, both are now in the form of a common denominator, and the addition of the two fractions can be completed:

$$\frac{1}{3} + \frac{1}{4} = \frac{3}{12} + \frac{4}{12} = \frac{7}{12}$$

Notice that this result is exactly analogous to the simple diagram above. Common denominator fractions need not be simplified with this type of diagram, but it is a valuable example to explain the principle. The common denominator is required whenever adding or subtracting fractions with different denominators. If the denominators are the same, then the addition or subtraction of numerators is all that is required. If more assistance is needed on how to find common denominators, the Arithmetic Reasoning chapter in Module 1 will provide information on finding the Least Common Multiple, or the lowest common denominator, required for addition and subtraction. Remember that the individual fractions will retain the same value only if the numerator and denominator are multiplied by the same value.

Multiplication of fractions is a simple operation because fractions multiply as follows:

$$\frac{7}{8} * \frac{3}{4} = \frac{(7*3)}{(8*4)} = \frac{21}{32}$$

This fraction is in its simplest form because there are no common factors. If common factors exist in the numerator and denominator of a fraction, then that fraction must be simplified.

Division of fractions should never be attempted in the form of a ratio. The method is confusing, elaborate and unreliable in a testing situation. Instead, every fraction division problem is a simple operation because the division operation can be rewritten as a multiplication operation. To begin, as stated previously:

dividend / divisor = quotient
This can be rewritten as:
dividend * ($\frac{1}{divisor}$) = quotient

This yields exactly the same outcome as division. The quantity ($\frac{1}{divisor}$) is called a reciprocal, and for a fraction, it's as simple as flipping the fraction upside down. Therefore:

$$(\tfrac{5}{8}) / (\tfrac{1}{4}) = \frac{5}{8} * \frac{4}{1} = \frac{20}{32} = \frac{5}{8} \text{ (in simplified form)}$$

Fraction to Decimal Conversions

Every fraction represents a division problem. The decimal value of any fraction is represented by the numerator, (top value), divided by the denominator (bottom value). Certain combinations, such as $\frac{1}{3}$, will result in repeating decimals that will always be

rounded in a multiple-choice testing situation.

The fraction $\frac{1}{2}$ has a decimal value of 0.5, which is the value of 1 divided by 2. The values of improper fractions such as $\frac{3}{2}$, $\frac{5}{2}$, or $\frac{7}{2}$ (larger numerator than denominator) are determined by dividing as previously stated or more easily by multiplying the numerator by 0.5. So the improper fraction of $\frac{7}{2}$ is 7 * 0.5, or 3.5. Often, the determination of the unit fraction (1 divided by the denominator) followed by the decimal multiplication is simpler in a testing situation.

The fraction $\frac{3}{5}$ has a decimal value of 0.6, which is the value of 3 divided by 5. Alternately, the value of the unit fraction of $\frac{1}{5}$ is 0.2, and that unit fraction multiplied by 3 is 0.6. If you know the unit fractions for common fraction values, the answer selection process may be simplified.

When a fraction such as $\frac{5}{7}$ is evaluated, the quotient of 5 divided by 7 results in a lengthy decimal value of 0.71428.... That extended value will never appear as a multiple-choice test answer selection. Typically, that value will be rounded to either 0.71 or 0.714. Remember that testing instructions say to choose the best answer. Your best choice may be a rounded number.

Decimal to Fraction Conversions

All decimals are also fractions and can be written in that form. The fractions that result all have powers of 10 in the denominator and usually need to be simplified in order to be compared to multiple-choice answers in a testing situation.

For example, simple decimal values, such as 0.25, can be written as the fraction $\frac{25}{100}$. This fraction must be simplified to be correct. $\frac{25}{100}$ can be rewritten as a product:

$$\frac{(25 * 1)}{(25 * 4)}$$
or
$$\frac{25}{25} * \frac{1}{4}$$

The fraction can be expressed correctly as $\frac{1}{4}$ since the fraction $\frac{25}{25}$ is simplified to 1. Recognizing the common factors in the numerator and denominator is the essential element in making these conversions.

For testing purposes, decimal conversions will often be based on common fraction values. For example, $1/_{16}$, if divided with long division, is 0.0625. Any integer multiple of this value results in a fraction with 16 in the denominator.

The value 0.0625 is first rewritten as the fraction:

625/10000

Simplifying with factors of 5 in the numerator and denominator gives the fraction:

125/2000

Simplifying with factors of 25 in the numerator and denominator gives the fraction:

5/80

Simplifying with factors of 5 in the numerator and denominator one more time gives the simplified fraction:

1/16

While either of these methods may require an extra amount of time to complete, usually the answer choices may be logically reduced to two of the four examples. Testing the answer choices is simply a matter of multiplying the decimal value by the denominator to determine if the numerator is correct.

Another solution method, logical deduction, can be used as a simple, reliable and time saving approach to finding the fractional value of 0.435. In this example, the following is a list of possible multiple-choice answers:

A   3/16
B   5/16
C   7/16
D   9/16

Logically, any fraction greater than $1/_2$ is immediately eliminated since:

0.435 < 0.5

So, first eliminate answer D. Incorrect answer choices will be eliminated with this type of logical deduction. Second, notice that in the answer choice:

3/16 < 1/4

and in decimal form

3/16 < 0.25

So, choice A can logically be eliminated since our answer comparison is with 0.435.

Third, notice that in the answer choices:

5/16 > 1/4

and in decimal form

5/16 > 0.25

Since $5/_{16}$ is just slightly more than $1/_4$, choice B can be eliminated since our comparison is with 0.435.

Finally, C is chosen as the most likely answer choice. It is the logical choice since:

7/16 < 1/2

and

0.435 < 0.5

PERCENTAGES

Percentages is a concept you are most likely familiar with from real-world applications, so these are some of the less scary math problems that appear on tests. However, test writers take that confidence into account and can use it against you, so it's important to be careful on problems with percentages. Let's look at an example:

A sweater went on sale and now costs $25.20. If the original price was $42.00, what is the percent discount?

16.8%
20.0%
25.0%
40.0%
60.0%

Take a minute to work out the problem for yourself. If you get the wrong answer, it will be helpful to you to see where you went wrong – several of the answer choices are distinct traps that often appear on test questions like this.

SOLUTION:

With percentages, you can always set up a fraction.

First, you want to know what percent the sale price is of the original price. The reference point, or original price, will go on the bottom of the fraction. The numerator will be the sale price. The ratio of 25.2 / 42 is equal to 6 / 10.

The sale price, $25.20, is 0.6, or 60%, of the original price. A percentage is just the decimal times 100%. This is answer choice E. However, the question did NOT ask what percent the new price is of the original price. Read carefully: it asks for the percent *discount*. This language is commonly used for questions with prices. Here's what it means, in math terms:

Percentage discount = 100% - Percentage of the Sale Price

The percent discount is the amount less than 100% that the sale price is of the original price. We can use this equation to solve, which yields:

$$(42 - 25.2) / 42 = 0.40$$

Remember, a percent is a decimal times 100%. So, we can convert the decimal on the right side to a percentage by multiplying by 100%:

$$100\% * 0.40 = 40\%$$

The sale price is 40% *less than* the original price, which is answer choice D. Another mathematical reasoning approach would be to take the original fraction subtracted from 1:

$$1 - 25.2 / 42 = 0.4$$

From here, just recognize that if the sale price *is* 60% of the original price, then it is 40% *less than* the original price.

You can solve for the discounted amount and then find that as a percent of the original amount to solve for the percentage of the discount:

$$42 - 25.2 = 16.80$$
$$16.80 / 42 = 0.4$$

Those are three different ways to approach one problem, using the same concept of percentage and

recognizing that a percent *discount* requires subtraction from the original. Here's another percentage problem, this time with a different trick:

168 is 120% of what number?

Solution:
First, convert 120% to a decimal. Remember, converting a percentage to a decimal is done by dividing by 100%:

$$120 / 100 = 1.2$$

We are told that 168 is this percent *of* some other number. This means that 168 goes in the numerator of our percent fraction equation. Here is the resulting equation:

$$168 / x = 1.2$$

Here, *x* signifies the unknown number in the problem. Writing the percent equation is indispensable to solving this type of problem. Multiply both sides by *x* and then divide both sides by 1.2 to isolate the variable:

$$168(x) / x = 1.2(x)$$
$$168 = 1.2x$$
$$168 / 1.2 = 1.2x / 1.2$$
$$140 = x$$

Therefore, 168 is 120% of 140. We can verify this answer by plugging the numbers back into the original equation:

$$168 / 140 = 1.2$$

This problem is tricky because the percentage is greater than 100%, or greater than 1.0, so it violates our intuition that the bigger number should go on the bottom of the fraction. Usually, percentages are less than 100. However, when percentages are larger than 100, the numerator is bigger than the denominator. The inverse of this question could be the following:

168 is what percent of 140?

Many people, after reading this question, would automatically set up the following fraction equation:

$$140/168 = 0.83$$

83% would likely be an answer choice, but it's the wrong answer. The question is asking for 168 / 140. Read these questions carefully, and don't automatically place the larger number in the denominator.

Let's look at one more example, which combines these concepts, and then do a couple practice problems:
An ingredient in a recipe is decreased by 20%. By what percentage does the new amount need to be increased to obtain the original amount of the ingredient?

SOLUTION:

Here is a pro's tip for working with percentages:

When a problem is given only in percentages with no given numbers, you can substitute in any value to work with as your original amount. Since you are solving for a percent, you'll get the same answer no matter what numbers are used because percentages are ratios. The easiest number to work with in problems like this is 100, so use that as the original recipe amount. 100 what? Cups of flour? Chicken tenders? Chocolate chips? Doesn't matter. Here's how your equation should look:

$$x / 100 = 0.20$$

Solve for x, which gives the amount the ingredient has been decreased by:

$$x = 100 * 0.20$$

Remember that 20% is a decimal, so $0.20 * 100 = 20$. The ingredient has been decreased by 20 units. What is the new amount?

$$100 - 20 = 80$$

What was the question asking for? *By what percent does the new amount need to be increased to obtain the original amount of the ingredient?* Let's parse this mathematical language. We've found the new amount of the ingredient, 80. The original amount, we decided, was 100.

The next step in answering the question is to find the *amount* that we would need to add to get back to the original amount. This part is pretty easy:

$$80 + x = 100$$
$$x = 20$$

It's the same amount that we subtracted from the original amount, 20. But the question asks what percentage of 80 is required to add 20?

Set up the percentage equation. 80 times what percent (x / 100) will give that extra 20 units?

$$80 * x / 100 = 20$$

Solve as normal by dividing both sides by 80 and then multiplying both sides by 100:

$$x / 100 = 0.25$$
$$x = 25$$

The new amount must be increased by 25% to equal the original amount.

MATHEMATICS KNOWLEDGE

Rates and Systems of Equations

These are some of the most common questions on standardized math exams and also some of the most criticized. How many pop culture references are there to the nightmare of the "if train A is traveling west of Detroit at 70 miles an hour and train B is traveling north of Denver at 90 miles an hour, what is the weight of the moon" variety? Excluding the nonsensical nature of the joke (would we weigh the moon in terms of its own gravity, or Earth's? Do bodies in orbit actually weigh *anything*?? Wait, wrong subject), this is simply a rate problem! Train A has a speed and a direction, Train B has a speed and a direction, and given those facts, you can answer all kinds of questions easily.

A *rate* is anything that relates two types of measurement: distance and time, dollars and workers,

mass and volume, x per y. Exchange rates tell us how much of one currency you can get for a certain amount of another currency. Speedometers tell us how many miles we travel per unit of time. Growth rates tell us how much additional population we get over time. Rates are everywhere in the world, and they are everywhere on standardized math tests. To express a rate mathematically, think of the following:

All rates express one measurement *in terms of* another.

For example, *miles per hour* gives us a measurement of distance (miles) for one unit of time (an hour). "Per" is a term that means divide. It looks like this:

If a car is traveling 70 mph, it goes 70 miles for every one hour of time that passes.

All rates work this way. If you can get €0.81 (Euros) for one American dollar, the exchange rate is:

€0.81 (Euros) / 1 Dollar = 0.81 Euros per Dollar

A rate is written as a fraction. A rate *equation* gives you a value of one of the measurements if you know the rate and the value of the other measurement.

If a car travels 70 mph: Distance = 70 miles/hour * hours
This recipe for the equation always works for a rate problem:

Examine the mph example: when you multiply 70 miles/hour times a number of hours, the hours units cancel out, leaving you with a number of miles. This works for any type of rate. The thing being measured on the *top* (numerator) of the rate measurement is equal to the rate times the unit being measured on the *bottom* of the rate measurement.

To SOLVE A RATE PROBLEM, FOLLOW THESE STEPS:

1. Read the question carefully to determine what you will be solving for. Is it an amount of time? A distance? Something else? Make sure you understand this before anything else. It can be helpful to name the variables at this point.

2. **Write equations to express all of the information given in the problem.** This is just like we've demonstrated for percentage problems, averaging problems, etc. The ability to express information in an equation is one of the main mathematical reasoning abilities that you can demonstrate to succeed on tests like these. Remember the equation:
Distance = Rate * Time

3. **Solve!**
First, a simple example:

A train is traveling west at 75 mph. How long will it take to travel 60 miles?

Step 1: Identify what the question is asking for: in this instance, it's *how long*, or the time it takes to travel 60 miles.

Step 2: Write an equation: 60 = 75 * time

Step 3: Solve! We know that the rate is 75 miles per hour and that the miles traveled is 60. To solve for time, just plug those values into the equation:

Isolate the "x hours" by dividing both sides by 75 mph:

60 miles / 75 miles per hour = 0.8 hours
0.8 hours * 60 minutes per hour = 48 minutes

Rate problems can also require a system of equations. This just means that you need to write two equations to relate two unknown variables, instead of one equation to solve for one unknown variable, like the problem above. The algebra is not any more difficult for these types of problems. They just require the extra step of writing another equation.

For example: Jessica assembles one model airplane per hour. James assembles one model airplane per 45 minutes. If they work for the same amount of time and assemble twelve planes all together, how many planes did James assemble?

Step 1: Identify what the question is asking for: the number of planes that James assembled.

Step 2: Write equations:

x = 1 Airplanes per hour * T hours
y = 1/0.75 Airplanes per hour * T hours
x + y = 12

You convert "45 minutes" to 0.75 hours, since 45/60 = 0.75. If you'd rather not do that, you could leave the rate in minutes, but then change Jessica's rate to 60 minutes instead of one hour. The important thing is to use the same units for time across the whole equation.

Step 3: Solve! Notice that the "T hours" term is the same in both of the rate equations. The problem stated that the two of them worked for the same amount of time. To solve for the number of planes

James assembled, first we need to find T hours. The *number of planes Jessica assembles* and the *number of planes James assembles* can be added together since we know that the sum is 12. This is the new equation from adding those together:

12 = 1 Airplanes per hour * T hours + 1/0.75
Airplanes per hour * T hours

The algebra here is a little bit hairy, but we can handle it! To solve for time, isolate T step by step. First, multiply every term in the equation by "1 hour":

Now, the unit "hour" cancels out of both terms on the right side of the equation. Remember, when you multiply *and* divide a term by something, that cancels out:

Now, we have:

12 plane hours = 1 plane * T hours + 1/0.75 * T hours

We need to isolate "T hours." Gather together the "T hours" terms on the right side of the equation. Right now, they are separated into an addition expression. If we add them together, they will be collected into one term. Since 1/0.75 is equal to 4/3, change that term first:

12 plane hours = 1 plane * T hours + 4/3 plane * T hours

Now add:

12 plane hours = (1 plane + 4/3 plane) * T hours
12 plane hours = (1 and 4/3 plane) * T hours

You add together 1 and 4/3. This is the same as saying that $1x + 2x = 3x$. We just collected the like terms.

Now, divide both sides by 1 plane to isolate the T hours term. Since mixed fractions are difficult to work with, change this into an improper fraction:

12 plane hours = (7/3 plane) * T hours

The planes unit cancels out on the right side. So we are left with:

12 hours / (7/3) = T hours

One arithmetic trick: dividing by a fraction is the same as multiplying by the inverse of the fraction. If you are comfortable dividing by fractions on your calculator, you can do the rest of the problem that way, or else you can flip the fraction over and simplify the arithmetic:

12 * 3/7 = T hours
36/7 = T hours
5 1/7 = T hours

The answer is $x = 5 \frac{1}{7}$ hours, or approximately 5.14 hours.

That was a long problem! But it included rates, a system of equations, unit conversions (changing minutes into fractions of an hour) and algebra with complex fractions. That is about the most difficult type of rate problem you would ever see on a standardized math exam, so if you were able to follow along with the solution you're in good shape.

Remember, on exams like this, the vast majority of points come from the easier problems. The harder problems (which on most exams tend to be at the end of a section) are always worth giving a shot, but they are not necessary to get a good score. Problems like these are great for practice because they include a lot of different concepts. Don't be discouraged if you don't always get the tougher problems correct on the first try. They are preparing you to do well on a wide range of different problem types!

MODULE 3

DAY, LOCATION, MUSIC

1

MONDAY, OCTOBER 12

COFFEE SHOP ON MAIN STREET

MY FAVORITE BAND

2

3

VOCABULARY

LET'S FACE IT. VOCABULARY JUST ISN'T THAT INTERESTING. SO, LET'S CHANGE IT UP! BELOW IS
A CROSSWORD PUZZLE TO HELP YOU LEARN SOME NEW WORDS AND EXPAND YOUR VOCABULARY.

abhorrent bar chide debonair err frail glut haughty immerse jargon lofty malign abscond
obscure parity ravage slander transpose unison vague amity ambiguous carcass hoist
perpetual surmount

Across

3. to leave quickly
7. destroy or ruin
8. weak
11. together or at once
13. of considerable height
15. to overcome something
16. disgusting or hateful
19. stylish and charming
20. speaking falsely about someone
23. having more than one explanation
24. unclear or uncertain
25. to make a mistake
26. a state of being without change

Down

1. cover completely
2. specialized words
4. relatively unknown
5. arrogant
6. too much of something
9. friendly relations between two people
10. raise with a mechanical device
12. the remains of a dead animal
14. to change an arrangement
17. speak badly about
18. to scold
21. the equivalent of something
22. forbid or prevent

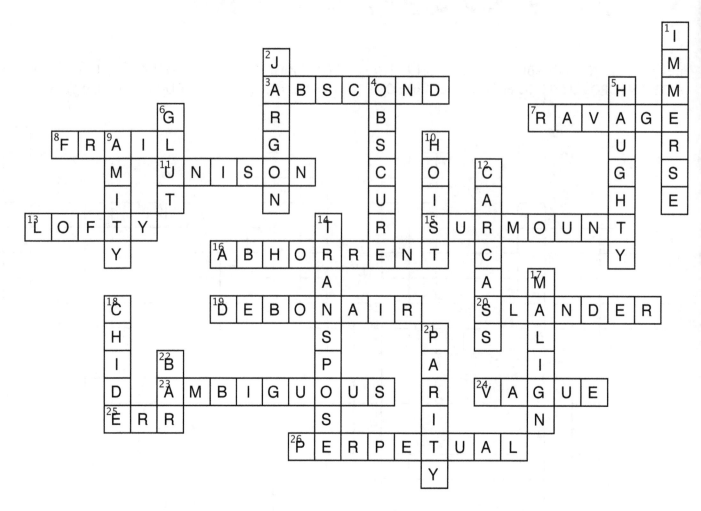

abhorrent bar chide debonair err frail glut haughty immerse jargon lofty malign abscond obscure parity ravage slander transpose unison vague amity ambiguous carcass hoist perpetual surmount

Across

3. to leave quickly [ABSCOND]
7. destroy or ruin [RAVAGE]
8. weak [FRAIL]
11. together or at once [UNISON]
13. of considerable height [LOFTY]
15. to overcome something [SURMOUNT]
16. disgusting or hateful [ABHORRENT]
19. stylish and charming [DEBONAIR]
20. speaking falsely about someone [SLANDER]
23. having more than one explanation [AMBIGUOUS]
24. unclear or uncertain [VAGUE]
25. to make a mistake [ERR]
26. a state of being without change [PERPETUAL]

Down

1. cover completely [IMMERSE]
2. specialized words [JARGON]
4. relatively unknown [OBSCURE]
5. arrogant [HAUGHTY]
6. too much of something [GLUT]
9. friendly relations between two people [AMITY]
10. raise with a mechanical device [HOIST]
12. the remains of a dead animal [CARCASS]
14. to change an arrangement [TRANSPOSE]
17. speak badly about [MALIGN]
18. to scold [CHIDE]
21. the equivalent of something [PARITY]
22. forbid or prevent [BAR]

CRITICAL READING

INFERENCES AND HOW TO MAKE THEM AND USE THEM

*Inference is a mental process by which you reach a conclusion based on specific evidence. Inferences are the stock and trade of detectives examining clues, of doctors diagnosing diseases, and of car mechanics repairing engines. We infer motives, purpose and intentions.

You use inference every day. You interpret actions to be examples of behavioral characteristics, intents or expressions of particular feelings. You infer it is raining when you see someone with an open umbrella. You infer that people are thirsty if they ask for a glass of water. You infer that evidence in a text is authoritative when it is attributed to a scholar in that particular field.

You want to find significance. You listen to remarks and want to make sense of them. What might the speaker mean? Why is he or she saying that? You must go beyond specific remarks to determine underlying significance or broader meaning. When you read that someone cheated on his or her income taxes, you might take that as an example of financial ingenuity,

daring or stupidity. You seek purposes and reasons.

Inferences are not random. While they may come about mysteriously with sudden recognition, you usually make inferences very orderly. Inferences may be guesses, but they are educated guesses based on supporting evidence. The evidence requires that you reach a specific conclusion.

Inferences are not achieved with mathematical rigor, and they do not have the certainty obtained with deductive reasoning. Inferences tend to reflect prior knowledge and experience as well as personal beliefs and assumptions. Thus, inferences tend to reflect your stake in a situation or your interests in the outcome. People may reason differently or bring different assumptions or premises to bear. This is why bias is addressed so carefully in our criminal justice system, so defendants are given a fair trial.

EXAMPLE
Given evidence that polychlorinated biphenyls (PCB) cause cancer in people and that PCB's are in a particular water system, all reasonable people would reach the conclusion that the water system is

dangerous to people. But, given evidence that there is an increase in skin cancer among people who sun bathe, not all people would conclude that sunbathing causes skin cancer. Sun bathing, they might argue, may be coincidental with exposure to other cancer-causing factors.

*Daniel J. Kurland
(www.criticalreading.com/inference_process.htm)

Inference Questions

Inference questions ask about ideas that are not directly stated, but rather are implied by the passage. They ask you to draw conclusions based on the information in the passage. Inference questions usually include words like "imply," "infer" or "conclude," or they may ask you what the author "would probably" think or do in a given situation based on what was stated in the passage.

With inference questions, it is important not to go *too far* beyond the scope of the passage. You are not expected to make any guesses. There is a single correct answer that is a logical, next-step conclusion from what is presented in the passage.

Let's take a look at some sample inference questions. Read through the following passages and use your inference skills to answer the questions. Remember that the inferences you make are not always obvious or directly stated in the passage.

SAMPLE 1

"Despite the fact that the practice is illegal in many states, some people set off their own fireworks at home each summer, especially on Independence Day. Most cities have public fireworks displays run by experienced professionals in a controlled environment, but many people still enjoy the thrill of setting off their own fireworks. However, this practice can be dangerous, and many people are injured each year from fireworks-related accidents. Having Independence Day fireworks in your own backyard is not worth the safety risk, especially when public fireworks displays are available in most areas."

The author of this passage would most likely support:

A. The complete legalization of fireworks nationwide
B. The reduction of public fireworks displays
C. More rigorous enforcement of restrictions on home fireworks
D. Promoting home fireworks use

Answer: C

In the passage, the author takes a negative tone toward home fireworks use, citing the fact that the practice is dangerous, illegal in some areas and unnecessary since many areas have safe public fireworks displays on holidays. Someone who is critical of home fireworks use would support strong enforcement of restrictions on their use.

SAMPLE 2

"A man took his car to the mechanic because the engine was overheating. The mechanic opened the hood to inspect the situation. He removed the radiator cap and could see that there was a sufficient amount of coolant in the radiator. He took the car for a drive and also noticed that the engine would overheat at a stoplight, but not on the highway."

According to the passage, what can you infer about the engine?

A. The engine needs to be replaced
B. The radiator is leaking
C. The engine is operating normally
D. The radiator fan is broken

Answer: D

Although an overheating engine does indicate an abnormal condition, it does not necessarily indicate a catastrophic failure. Thus, the engine can be repaired instead of replaced. The radiator was full of coolant, so that eliminates the possibility of a leak. When a vehicle is moving, the airflow across the radiator cools the coolant. However, when a vehicle is stationary, the fan is responsible for cooling the coolant. If the fan is not working correctly, this would explain the overheating at a stoplight, but not on the highway.

ARITHMETIC REASONING

WORKING WITH SETS

All standardized math exams will touch on the basic statistical descriptions of sets of numbers: mean (the same as an average, for a set), median, mode and range. These are terms to know. Let's look at an example set and examine what each of these terms means:

Set of numbers: 42, 18, 21, 26, 22, 21

MEAN/AVERAGE

The mean of a set of numbers is the average value of the set. The formula for finding the mean is:

$$\frac{\text{sum of the numbers in the set}}{\text{quantity of numbers in the set}} = \text{mean}$$

Use this formula to find the mean of the example set:

$$\frac{42+18+21+26+22+21}{6} = \frac{150}{6} = 25$$

You add together all the numbers that appear in the set, and then divide by the quantity of numbers in the set. The mean, or average, value in the set is 25. Notice that the mean is not necessarily a number that appears in the set, although it can be.

MEDIAN

The median of a set is the number that appears in the middle when the set is ordered from least to greatest. Therefore, the first step in finding the mean is to put the numbers in the correct order, if they are not already. You should always do this physically, on your scratch paper, to make sure that you don't leave any numbers out of the reordering. For the example set, that would be:

$$18, 21, 21, 22, 26, 42$$

Make sure you've included all the numbers in the order, even if there are duplicates. If a set with a lot of numbers, it's helpful to cross them off in the original set as you order them on your scratch paper. This helps ensure that you don't leave one out.

If there is an odd quantity of numbers in the set, the median will be the middle number. For example, if a set is comprised of nine numbers, the median will be the fifth number of the ordered set.

However, the example set has six numbers. Since no single number is in the exact middle, we average the two middle numbers to find the median:

$$\frac{21+22}{2} = 21.5$$

The median of this set is 21.5.

MODE

The mode of a set of numbers is the number that appears most often. Speakers of French will find this easy to remember: *mode* is the French word for style. The number that appears the most is "in style" for this particular set.

The example set has one number that appears more than once: 21. Therefore, 21 is the mode. Sometimes, it's easiest to see this after the set is ordered, when duplicate numbers appear next to one another.

If a set has two numbers that equally appear most often, such as two 21s and two 22s, then both 21 *and* 22 are the mode. We don't average them together, as we do to find the median. Therefore, the mode is the only descriptor of a set that must always be a number in the set. Since there are two modes, the set would be described as "bimodal."

RANGE

The range of a set of numbers is the distance between the highest and lowest values. Once you've reordered a set, these values are easy to identify. Simply subtract the two values to get the range:

$$highest\ value - lowest\ value = range$$

For the example set, this would be:

$$42 - 18 = 24$$

The range of the set is 24.

Sets can include negative numbers, decimals, fractions, duplicates, etc. They may also appear in table form. Let's look at another example set to see what kinds of tricky questions you may encounter.

Month	Rainfall (inches)
August	0.8
September	1.3
October	2.1
November	1.3
December	3.7

What is the average rainfall for the months September, October, November and December?

SOLUTION:
Notice the first trick in this question – you are asked for the average of only four months, not all five listed in the table. This introduces two possible sources of error – you could add all five months' rainfall and/or divide by five when calculating the average. To find the average of only the four months stated in the question, the solution is:

$$\frac{1.3+2.1+1.3+3.7}{4} = 2.1\ inches$$

Here's another question for the same data table, but it uses a different approach to averaging:

The average monthly rainfall from July

through December was 1.7 inches. What was the rainfall, in inches, in July?

SOLUTION:
This question gives you the average and asks you to find the missing rainfall value. This is a common way to make a mean/average problem a little tricky for the average (mean) test-taker. You can solve these types of questions by applying the basic equation for finding the mean:

$$\frac{\text{sum of the numbers in the set}}{\text{quantity of numbers in the set}} = \text{mean}$$

Next, fill in all the known values:

$$\frac{\text{July}+0.8+1.3+2.1+1.3+3.7}{6} = 1.7$$

Solve algebraically:

$$\text{July}+0.8+1.3+2.1+1.3+3.7 = 1.7 * 6$$
$$\text{July} = (1.7 * 6)-0.8-1.3-2.1-1.3-3.7$$
$$\text{July} = 1 \text{ inch}$$

Now, try to solve this question:

What is the difference between the mode and the median of the rainfalls for August through December?

SOLUTION:
Simply find the mode and median values. Remember, the first step is to order the set:

$$0.8, 1.3, 1.3, 2.1, 3.7$$

The mode is 1.3 because that is the only number that appears more than once.

The median is 1.3 because, of the five numbers in the set, 1.3 is the third (middle) number.

Therefore, the difference between the mode and the median is:

$$1.3\text{-}1.3 = 0$$

MATHEMATICS KNOWLEDGE

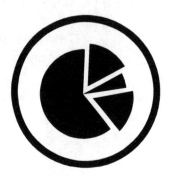

PROBABILITY

Every probability is a ratio as described below.

Probability =

$$\text{Probability} = \frac{\text{Total number of desired events}}{\text{Total number of possible outcomes}}$$

The simplest example of this type of ratio is found when tossing a coin. There are always two total outcomes, heads and tails, so the probability of either a head or a tail is always 1/2 for that coin.

Similarly, if you tossed that same coin 14 times, you would expect to see it land 7 times with the head showing and 7 times with the tail showing. Because these events are totally random, flipping the coin 14 times will not always provide an equal number of outcomes in a group of trials. So we say that the number of heads in a trial of 14 is the "expected value" of 7. Similarly, 7 would be the "expected value" for tails.

A common misconception is that there "has to be" a certain outcome based on the number of outcomes that have already occurred. In the repeated trial of an event, each outcome is it's own trial and is not influenced by the previous trial or trials.

The other common type of probability problem is with dice, where each of six faces of a cube has its own number from 1 to 6. Each of these numbers has the probability of 1/6 for a single roll of the die.

If we formulate a table of outcomes for two dice, thrown together, the details are slightly different. In this table, the individual numbers are shown across the top and vertically along the side. The entries in the table represent the total of the two dice.

	1	2	3	4	5	6	Cube "A"
1	2	3	4	5	6	7	
2	3	4	5	6	7	8	
3	4	5	6	7	8	9	
4	5	6	7	8	9	10	
5	6	7	8	9	10	11	
6	7	8	9	10	11	12	

Cube "B"

A look at the table shows that there are 36 possible outcomes when two dice are thrown together (6 * 6). The individual probabilities are shown below.

P (1) =	0		(never appears)
P (2) =	$1/36$ does not simplify		(appears once)
P (3) =	$2/36$	simplifies to $1/18$	(appears twice)
P (4) =	$3/36$	simplifies to $1/12$	(appears three times)
P (5) =	$4/36$	simplifies to $1/9$	(appears four times)
P (6) =	$5/36$	does not simplify	(appears five times)
P (7) =	$6/36$	simplifies to $1/6$	(appears six times)
P (8) =	$5/36$	does not simplify	(appears five times)
P (9) =	$4/36$	simplifies to $1/9$	(appears four times)
P (10) =	$3/36$	simplifies to $1/12$	(appears three times)
P (11) =	$2/36$	simplifies to $1/18$	(appears twice)
P (12) =	$1/36$	does not simplify	(appears once)
P (13) =	0		(never occurs)

The symmetry of the table helps us visualize the probability ratios for the individual outcomes. By the definition of probability, any number larger than 13 will never appear in the table so the probability has to be zero. The probability of any impossible outcome always has to be zero. By the same reasoning, any event that must happen will have a probability of one. So, the probability of rolling a number from 2 to 12 is one.

If you are finding the probability of two events happening, the individual probabilities are added. For example, the probability of rolling a ten or eleven is the same as the probability of rolling an eight. The number eight appears in the table the same number of times as the combined total of appearances of ten or eleven.

The formulation of ratios for probabilities is simplest when using fractions. Often, the expression of a probability answer will be in a percent or a decimal. A coin from the first example would have the following probabilities P (heads) = 50% or .5 or 0.5.

Formulating probabilities from a word problem can always be structured around the ratio defined at the beginning of this section. However the words can mislead or misdirect problem-solving efforts.

For example, a problem that describes a class distribution may often be stated as the number of boys and the number of girls. The probability of selecting a boy in a random sample is defined as the number of boys divided by the TOTAL number of boys AND girls.

This is simple to see, but problems can be worded to mislead you into selecting the incorrect answer or to lead to the wrong conclusion when calculating an answer.

Another way that probability problems can be misleading is when multiple choices are used when simplified ratios are required. For example, if a class is made up of 6 girls and 10 boys, the probability of randomly selecting a girl from the classroom is $^6/_{16}$ or $^3/_8$. The misleading multiple choices that may be listed would often include 60%, (6/10) or 50% (since there are two outcomes — boys and girls). Reading a probability problem carefully is extremely important in both formulating the probability ratio and in making sure that the correct ratio is selected in the correct form. If the probability ratio for the example is formulated as $^6/_{16}$, the simplified form of $^3/_8$ is the only correct answer.

RATIOS AND PROPORTIONS

Ratios and fractions are synonymous when discussing numerical values. The ratios or fractions always imply division of the numerator by the denominator. In this section, the discussion is directed toward how words appear in ratio problems and how those words should be interpreted.

A commonly used ratio is contained in the term "miles per hour", usually abbreviated by mph. When the term "miles per hour" is interpreted numerically, it is the ratio of the total number of miles traveled divided by the number of hours traveled. The key word in this commonly used term is "per". It literally means for each hour of travel, a specific number of miles will be traveled. It has the same implication when the term is "gallons per hour" (how fast a tub is filled or a lawn is watered) or "tons per year" (how much ore is mined in one year).

Another way that ratios can appear is when a phrase defines a ratio as one value to another. A commonly used comparison is usually the ratio of "men to women" or "boys to girls". When this terminology is used, the first term is in the numerator, and the second term is in the denominator by convention.

There is an inherent problem when this terminology is used as illustrated by the example below:

In a classroom setting, the ratio of girls to boys is 3 to 4 (or 3:4 in strictly mathematical terms). How many boys are there in the classroom if the total number of students is 28?

There are two ways that this word problem may be easily solved. If the ratio of ($girls/_{boys}$) is   , the actual numbers may be   or $^6/_8$ or $^9/_{12}$ or $^{12}/_{16}$ and so forth. These fractions are all equivalent fractions since they all simplify to the value of   . The equivalent fractions are easily determined as the ratios of multiples of the numerator and denominator of the original fraction. There is only one fraction where the numerator and denominator add to 28, and that is the ratio $^{12}/_{16}$. Therefore, the solution is the classroom has 16 boys and 12 girls.

Notice that the words specify which group (boys or girls) is the numerator and denominator in the original problem and in the solution. When choosing multiple-choice answers, make sure that the correct answer is chosen based upon the wording in the original problem. Most often, the correct ratio and its reciprocal are in the answer choices. For example, if the sample problem appeared on the exam, the multiple-choice answers would most likely include 16 boys and 12 girls AND 12 boys and 16 girls. But 16 boys and 12 girls is the correct answer choice.

MODULE 4

DAY, LOCATION, MUSIC

1

MONDAY, OCTOBER 12

COFFEE SHOP ON MAIN STREET

MY FAVORITE BAND

2

3

VOCABULARY

YOU COMPLETED A CROSSWORD PUZZLE FOR THE VOCABULARY CHAPTER IN MODULE 3. LET'S TRY ANOTHER ONE. BELOW IS A CROSSWORD PUZZLE TO HELP YOU LEARN SOME ADDITIONAL WORDS AND EXPAND YOUR VOCABULARY.

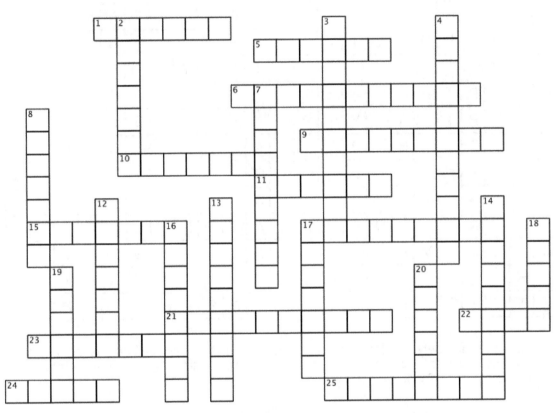

accost boggy canvass defy eccentric fidget hypocrite inertia jetty limber menagerie notary obliterate prestige reluctant spontaneous turmoil vestibule abdicate belligerent corrugated dilemma profane sublime thrift vagrant

Across

1. aggressively approach and speak to someone
5. flexible or supple
6. hostile and aggressive
9. unwilling or hesitant
10. moral or spiritual
11. a person authorized to perform legal formalities, usually relating to contracts or other documents
15. the mechanics principle where an object will remain in motion or at rest unless acted on by another force
17. a space adjacent to a main room or area
21. when a material is molded into a network of ridges and grooves
22. resist or refuse to obey
23. a difficult choice
24. a small pier at which boats can dock
25. deep respect and admiration

Down

2. to survey someone about his/her opinion
3. completely destroy
4. suddenly or instantly
7. somewhat strange or unconventional
8. a great disturbance or uncertainty
12. irreverent or disrespectful
13. someone who claims to have certain principles or beliefs, but does not act in the same manner
14. a strange collection of items
16. to renounce or fail to carry out
17. a person without a settled home
18. very wet and muddy
19. a characteristic of being wise with money
20. wiggle or squirm about

HOPEFULLY, THAT WASN'T TOO DIFFICULT. LET'S SEE HOW YOU DID!

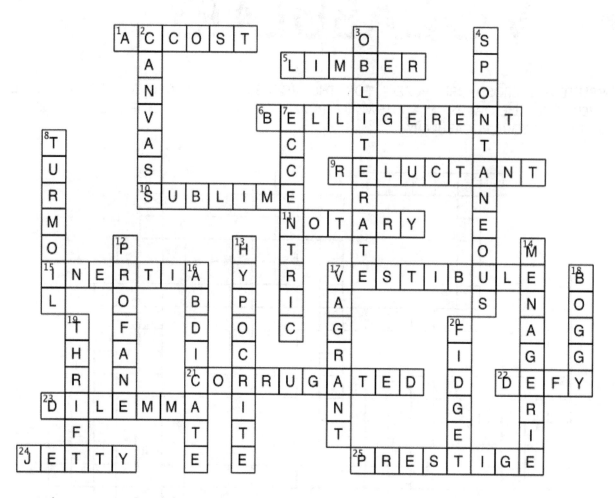

accost boggy canvass defy eccentric fidget hypocrite inertia jetty limber menagerie notary
obliterate prestige reluctant spontaneous turmoil vestibule abdicate belligerent corrugated
dilemma profane sublime thrift vagrant

Across

1. aggressively approach and speak to someone [ACCOST]
5. flexible or supple [LIMBER]
6. hostile and aggressive [BELLIGERENT]
9. unwilling or hesitant [RELUCTANT]
10. moral or spiritual [SUBLIME]
11. a person authorized to perform legal formalities, usually relating to contracts or other documents [NOTARY]
15. the mechanics principle where an object will remain in motion or at rest unless acted on by another force [INERTIA]
17. a space adjacent to a main room or area [VESTIBULE]
21. when a material is molded into a network of ridges and grooves [CORRUGATED]
22. resist or refuse to obey [DEFY]

Down

2. to survey someone about his/her opinion [CANVASS]
3. completely destroy [OBLITERATE]
4. suddenly or instantly [SPONTANEOUS]
7. somewhat strange or uncoventional [ECCENTRIC]
8. a great disturbance or uncertainty [TURMOIL]
12. irreverent or disrespectful [PROFANE]
13. someone who claims to have certain principles or beliefs, but does not act in the same manner [HYPOCRITE]
14. a strange collection of items [MENAGERIE]
16. to renounce or fail to carry out [ABDICATE]
17. a person without a settled home [VAGRANT]
18. very wet and muddy [BOGGY]
19. a characteristic of being wise with money [THRIFT]

CRITICAL READING

VOCABULARY-IN-CONTEXT

Vocabulary-in-Context questions ask you for the definition of a word as it is used within the context of the passage. The format of these questions is similar to that of Word Knowledge questions. You will be given a word and asked to select the closest meaning from a list of four choices. The difference, though, is that where Word Knowledge questions test straightforward vocabulary, the words chosen for Vocabulary-in-context questions are often words that can have more than one meaning. You will need to use context clues from the passage in order to figure out which meaning is correct.

It's also important to note that many questions on the exam will not always ask you to simply determine the meaning of a vocabulary word. Many times, instead of asking you for a synonym or definition of a vocabulary word, the question will ask you what the vocabulary word "most nearly means". For these types of questions, you'll need to use context clues and your existing vocabulary knowledge to determine which answer choice has a meaning that is closest to that of the vocabulary word.

To answer these questions, reread the sentence from the passage that the word is taken from. Come up with a prediction—your own definition or synonym of what the word means as used in that sentence. Then, look at the answer choices and choose the one that best matches your prediction. If you do not see your prediction among the answer choices, read each of the answer choices as part of the sentence, replacing the original word, and choose the one that makes the most sense.

Let's look at some examples.

Some of the questions you'll encounter will ask you to fill in the blank in a sentence. For the questions below, select the word that fits best in the sentence.

1. The bolt was _____. It took a lot of effort to loosen the fastener.

    A. Rusted
    B. Shiny
    C. Loose
    D. Strong

Answer: A.

Using the context clues in the sentence, you can assume that the missing word is somehow related to the phrase "loosen the fastener". Something about the bolt made it difficult to remove. You can immediately eliminate "shiny" since it is not related to the action of removing a fastener. Likewise, "loose" is not correct because if the bolt were loose, it wouldn't be difficult to remove it. "Strong" could possibly fit if there wasn't a better answer choice, but it's not typically used to describe how difficult a fastener is to remove. The word that best fits in the sentence is "rusted" because rust directly increases the difficulty of removing a fastener.

2. As the commanding officer's eyes widened and his face turned red, he proceeded to _____ the lance corporal.

    A. Tease
    B. Scold
    C. Compliment
    D. Correct

Answer: B.

Using the context clues in the sentence, you can assume that the missing word is somehow linked to widened eyes and a red face, which are associated with anger. You can immediately eliminate "tease" and "compliment" since those words connote lightheartedness and sincerity, not exactly similar to the demeanor described in the sentence. "Correct" could possibly fit if there wasn't a better answer

choice, but it's not necessarily associated with widened eyes and a red face. The word that best fits in the sentence is "scold" because scolding connotes anger or irritation, which correlate with widened eyes and a red face.

Sure, those were fairly easy, but those are just one type of vocabulary-in-context questions you'll probably encounter on the exam. For the questions below, select the word that MOST NEARLY means the same as the underlined word.

1. The chairman of the board abandoned his position after a damaging scandal.

A. Squandered
B. Resigned
C. Ignored
D. Neglected

Answer: B.

All the answer choices connote negative characteristics of the position of chairman of the board, but only "resigned" most closely matches the underlined word. "Squandered" suggests a wasted opportunity. "Ignored" means deliberately taking no notice of. "Neglected" signifies a failure to pay attention to. "Resigned" indicates voluntarily leaving a job, which MOST nearly means the same as "abandoned", leaving permanently.

2. Sarah considered herself a parsimonious shopper. She loved finding great shopping deals.
A. Cheap
B. Frugal
C. Economical
D. Thrifty

Answer: A.

All the answer choices reflect the general meaning of "parsimonious", being careful with money, but only one choice has a negative association. "Frugal", "economical" and "thrifty" are all adjectives with a positive connotation, but "cheap" is usually used as a negative description.

Those were a bit more difficult, but let's try a few more. For the questions below, select the word that LEAST LIKELY means the same as the underlined word.

1. The evidence of the murder was underlined destroyed before the trial.

A. Devastated
B. Obliterated
C. Ruined
D. Incinerated

Answer: D.

While all the answer choices can be used in place of "destroyed", "incinerated" suggests a specific type of damage: destruction by fire. Technically, "incinerated" is a logical answer, but the question isn't asking which choice is not logical. It's asking which choice LEAST likely means the underlined word. This was a tough one, but you should expect to see some questions like this on the exam.

2. While trying to negotiate a peace treaty, one side was being entirely underlined hostile to the other.

A. Belligerent
B. Threatening
C. Averse
D. Combative

Answer: C.

While all the choices are mostly synonyms of "hostile", only one choice excludes a violent implication in its definition. "Averse" means strongly opposed to, but "belligerent", "threatening" and "combative" all suggest harm or death, as does "hostile".

Sometimes, you will need to read a passage before answering the questions. Let's look at some examples of those questions.

"American elections consist of citizens voting for their government representatives. Today, this includes members of the U.S. Senate, but this was not always the case. When the United States Constitution was first written, the people did not get to elect their senators directly. Instead, the senators were appointed by state legislators (who are elected directly by the people in their respective states). This changed in 1913, however, with the 17th Amendment to the Constitution. This amendment allows for the direct election of U.S. Senators by the citizenry. While this election process can make the senators more accountable to their constituents, since the citizens will decide whether a senator will keep his or her job at the next election, it diminishes the voice that state legislatures have in the federal government."

1. The word underlined constituents in the passage most nearly means:

A. Elements
B. Employees
C. Senators
D. Voters

Answer: D.

By reading the choices back into the sentence, you can see that the best synonym for "constituents" is "voters". It is the voters who decide whether or not to reelect the senators. The word "constituents" on its own can have several meanings, including voters, elements, members, components and parts. In the context of this passage, however, "voters" is the best definition.

2. The word underlined amendment in the passage most nearly means:

A. Rule
B. Principle
C. Alteration
D. Truth

Answer: C.

By reading the choices back into the sentence, you can see that the best synonym for "amendment" is "alteration". The passage states how the Constitution originally provided for senator selection. However, the passage explains the difference in process after the 17th amendment. Because "alteration" means

ARITHMETIC REASONING

SCIENTIFIC NOTATION

Scientific notation was originally developed as a simplified way for scientists to express extremely large or small numbers. In mathematics, scientific notation is used to easily compare large and small numbers. Let's take a look at how to translate a real number to its scientific notation equivalent.

Converting standard numbers to scientific notation is performed without calculation, although counting place values is still essential. For example:

The number 2,345,000 is equal to 2.345 * 1,000,000. By writing the value of 1,000,000 as 106 (10 multiplied by itself 6 times), the formulation of the scientific notation equivalent of the original number is completed: 2.345 * 106.

Similarly, small decimal numbers can be written using scientific notation as well. For example:

The number 0.00736 is equal to 7.36 * 0.001. By writing the value of 0.001 as 10^{-3} (1 divided by 10, three times), the formulation of the scientific notation equivalent of the original number is completed: $7.36 * 10^{-3}$.

Instead dividing (or multiplying) by 10, the translation to scientific notation can also be simplified by counting the number of places that the decimal point is transferred in the conversion process. In the first example above, when the scientific notation was written, it began with writing 2.345. This number was formulated by moving the decimal point six places to the left in the original number. Therefore, the exponent of 10 was 6 (10^6).

Similarly, in the second example, the decimal part of the scientific notation number, 7.36, was written by moving the decimal point three places to the right. Therefore, the exponent of 10 was -3 (10^{-3}).

Using this method, no calculation is required. The included benefit is that the "significance" of numbers is easily determined. Answering the question of the number of significant figures for the two examples is a simple matter when using scientific notation. The number of digits in the decimal part of the scientific notation is always the number of significant figures. 2,345,000 has four significant figures. 0.00736 has three. The zeros in these numbers are often referred to as "place holders" when converting to scientific notation.

Notice that the exponent is NOT determined by counting zeros, but by counting the number of decimal places that are moved when formulating the scientific notation. The decimal part in scientific notation always has only one digit to the left of the decimal point.

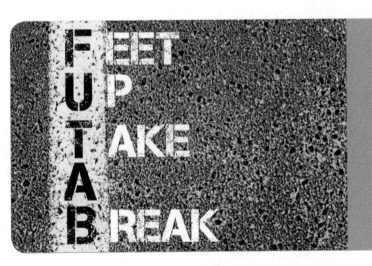

FEET UP TAKE A BREAK

BREAK TIME (15 Mins)

Perform an enjoyable activity to distract you from studying.
Read something light, go for a walk —
whatever you do, try to get
your mind off the material
for a little while.

MATHEMATICS KNOWLEDGE

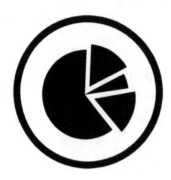

GEOMETRY

To tackle geometry questions on a mathematical reasoning test, there are a few formulas and rules that you need to know. This section takes you through those basic rules. It covers intersecting lines, triangles, squares and rectangles, and circles.

BASIC VOCABULARY

Vocabulary that is important to know for geometry questions includes the following:

LINE – A line is a set of all points between two endpoints. Lines have no area or width, only length.

ANGLE – An angle is the corner formed by two intersecting line segments, and it is measured in

degrees. Degrees measurements show the magnitude of the "sweep" of the angle. In the figure below, angle x is shown as the measure between the two line segments.

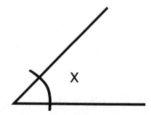

360° describes the angle measurement all the way around a full circle. Half of that, 180°, is the angle measurement across a straight line. Two lines at right angles to each other, called perpendicular lines, have an angle measurement of 90°.

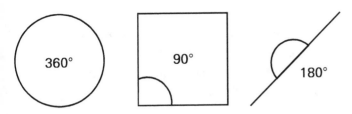

AREA – The area is the measure of space inside a two-dimensional figure. It has units of length * length, or length². For example, rooms are described as being a number of square feet. Counties are described as being so many square miles. Each basic shape has a special formula for determining area.

PERIMETER – The perimeter is the measure of the length around the outside of a figure.

VOLUME – For three-dimensional figures, the volume is the measure of space inside the figure. Volume has three dimensions: length * width * height. Because of this, it has units of length³ (cubic length). For example, you may have heard "cubic feet" used to describe the volume of something like a storage unit. This formula applies only to square and rectangular three-dimensional shapes. Other figures have their own formulas for determining volume.

INTERSECTING LINES

There are two important properties to know about pairs of intersecting lines:
1. They form angles that add up to 180° along the sides of each line.

2. They create two pairs of equal angles.

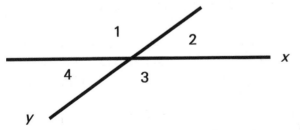

For example, in the diagram above, line x intersects line y, forming the four angles 1, 2, 3 and 4. Any two angles along one side of a line will add up to 180°:

$$Angle\ 1 + Angle\ 2 = 180°$$
$$Angle\ 2 + Angle\ 3 = 180°$$
$$Angle\ 3 + Angle\ 4 = 180°$$
$$Angle\ 4 + Angle\ 1 = 180°$$

All four of the angles added together would equal 360°:

$$Angle\ 1 + Angle\ 2 + Angle\ 3 + Angle\ 4 = 360°$$

The two angles DIAGONAL from each other must be equal. For the figure above, we know that:

$$Angle\ 1 = Angle\ 3$$
$$Angle\ 2 = Angle\ 4$$

This property is very useful: if you are given any one of the angles, you can immediately solve for the other three. If you are told that Angle 1 = 120°, then you know that Angle 2 = 180° - 120° = 60°. Since Angle 3 = Angle 1 and Angle 4 = Angle 2, you now know all four angles.

PARALLEL/PERPENDICULAR LINES

Parallel lines are lines that lie on the same 2-D plane (i.e., the page) and never intersect each other. The thing to remember about parallel lines is that if a line intersects two parallel lines, it will form a bunch of corresponding angles (like the ones discussed above). Also, you can never assume that two lines are parallel just from a diagram. You need to be told or given enough information that you can deduce it. Parallel lines have the same slope.

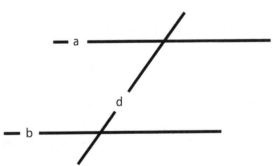

Lines a and b are parallel and are intersected by line d.

In the diagram above, all four of the acute angles (the ones smaller than 90°) are equal to each other. All four of the obtuse angles (the ones greater than 90°) are equal to each other. Why? Because a line intersecting parallel lines forms equivalent angles. This is simply an expanded case of the intersecting lines concept discussed earlier.

SQUARES AND RECTANGLES

By definition, a square has four sides of equal length and four angles of 90°. A rectangle has two pairs of sides of equal length and four angles of 90°. This means that the sum of all four angles in a square or rectangle is 360°.

In the diagram above, the shape on the left is a square. So, if you are given the length of side a, you automatically know the length of every side. You already know the measure of every angle, because they are all 90° - the measure of right (perpendicular) angles.

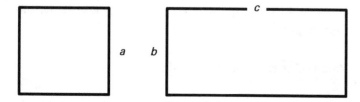

The shape on the right is a rectangle. So, if you are given the length of side b, you know the length of the opposite side. However, you do not know the length of the longer two sides unless they are given.

The perimeter of a square is the sum of all four line segments. Since the line segments are equal, the equation is as follows:

Perimeter of a square = 4 * (side length)

The perimeter of the square above is $4a$.

The perimeter of the rectangle is also the sum of its sides. However, since there are two pairs of equal length sides in a rectangle, the equation is as follows:

Perimeter of a rectangle =
2 * (long side length) + 2 * (short side length)

The perimeter of the rectangle above is $2b + 2c$.

The area of a square is its length times its width. Since length and width are the same for a square, the area is the length of one of its sides squared (that's where the term "squared" comes from) and the equation is as follows:

Area = a^2

For a rectangle, length times width is not equal to one side squared (it's not a square, so the sides are not all the same length). The equation for the area of a rectangle is as follows:

Area = $b * c$

TRIANGLES

A triangle is a polygon (closed shape) made of three line segments. While the four angles in a square and rectangle always add up to 360°, the three angles in a triangle always add up to 180°. However, these angles are not always the same measure, as they are for squares and rectangles.

Below are the different types of triangles:

| EQUILATERAL | ISOSCELES | RIGHT |
| SIDES OF SAME LENGTH | TWO SIDES OF SAME LENGTH TWO ANGLES OF SAME | ONE ANGLE OF 90° |

The area of a triangle will always equal one half of the product of its base and its height. You can choose any side to be the base (the one at the bottom of the triangle is probably best), and the height of a triangle is the perpendicular line from the base to the opposite angle. The height is NOT the length of a side, unless the triangle is a right triangle. For example:

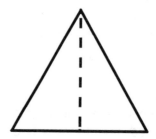

In this triangle, the bottom leg is the base, and the dotted line is the height.

A = 1/2 (base * height)

Another important formula to know when working with triangles is the Pythagorean Theorem. This tells you how to relate the lengths of the sides of right triangles – the ones that include 90° angles.

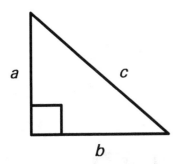

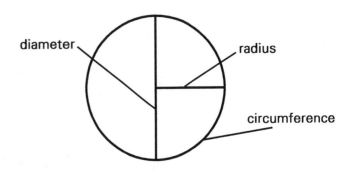

In the diagram above, you have right triangle ABC. You know it's a right triangle because it has a 90° angle – not because it *looks* like one. Never assume the measure of an angle without being given that information. Side c is called the hypotenuse, which is the longest side of a right triangle. Sides a, b and c are related to each other according to the Pythagorean Theorem:

$$c^2 = a^2 + b^2$$

Regardless of how the sides of the right triangle are labeled, the length of the longest side squared is equal to the sum of the lengths of the two shorter sides, each squared. There will likely be a few problems that will require you to use this relationship to solve.

Here are some important details to remember about triangles:

- A triangle has three sides and three angles.
- The angles of a triangle will always add up to 180°.
- A triangle is a "right triangle" if one of the angles is 90°.
- If a triangle is equilateral, all angles are 60°, and all sides are the same length.
- The area of a triangle is one half times the base times the height.
- For right triangles, you can relate the lengths of the sides using the Pythagorean Theorem.

CIRCLES

A circle is a figure without sides. Instead, it has a circumference with a set of points equidistant from the center of the circle.

Here are some important details to remember about circles:

- The measurement around the outside of a circle is called the circumference.
- The line segment going from the center of the circle to the circumference is called the radius.
- The line segment that goes across the entire circle, passing through the center, is the diameter.
- The number of degrees in the central angle of a circle is 360°.

The circumference of a circle can be found using the following formula:

$$C = 2\pi r$$

In this formula, r is the radius (or the distance from the center of the circle to an outside point on the circle). If you are given the diameter, then you can find the circumference using this formula:

$$C = \pi d$$

The radius is twice the length of the diameter:

$$D = 2r$$

The area of a circle can be found using this formula:

$$A = \pi r^2$$

So, the area is equal to the radius squared times the constant (pronounced pi). Sometimes, answer choices are given with as a part of the value, , for example. When you see this, work out the problem without substituting the value of (approximately 3.14). You can, in fact, estimate that is 3.14 or 22/7 in your calculations, but you'll end up with a decimal or fraction for your answer.

WRITING

Although writing is simply a physical extension of your mind's logical reasoning, it is not the easiest academic task to complete, especially when you're being timed. It can be intimidating to stare at a blank page, all the while knowing that you don't have much time to complete the task. However, it is one of the most important skills to have as you progress into higher education and your career. Writing an essay doesn't need to be difficult—in fact, there are specific ways to approach essays. If you understand these various strategies, you'll do just fine.

What to Expect

As part of the essay, you will be asked to evaluate and analyze the perspectives presented, state and develop your own unique perspective and then explain the relationship between your perspective and those presented. You may adopt a given perspective, either in part or in whole, or you may develop your own. The point of view you take on the issue will not affect your score.

Your essay will be scored based on your ability to do the following:

· Analyze and evaluate multiple perspectives on a complex issue
· State and develop your own perspective on the issue
· Explain and support your ideas with logical reasoning and detailed examples
· Clearly and logically organize your ideas in an essay
· Effectively communicate your ideas in standard written English

Sample Prompt

We spend our lives as workers. During our youngest years, we work to grow and to learn how to become self-sufficient. In school, we work to learn our studies and how we can relevantly apply them to our lives. As we become adults, we work to achieve, to feel accomplished and to support ourselves and our families.

Psychologists and philosophers throughout the ages have questioned what it is that motivates us, trying to determine what drives us toward achievement. What is it, they have asked, that makes us "tick"? These questions have led to several theories on how motivation works.

Read and carefully consider the following three motivational theories. Each suggests a particular means of how and why people are motivated in the workplace:

Perspective One- Hierarchy of Needs: Psychologist Abraham Maslow categorized human needs into 5 basic subsets: A need for basic survival such as food and water, for safety, for love, for esteem, and for self-actualization. Only when each of the lower level needs is satisfied can an individual pursue the fulfillment of a higher need. Employers hoping to motivate their workers can only do so if they understand the current need level of those they are trying to motivate. For instance, a person out of a job will be motivated by the need for basic survival. One who is gainfully employed but does not feel professionally fulfilled will be motivated by a need for esteem.

Perspective Two- Carrot and Stick: Philosopher Jeremy Bentham in the 1800's divided the concept of motivation into two basic categories: incentives and fear. Some workers, he argued, are motivated by a desire to achieve- more money, more status and/or power, or more acknowledgement and praise. Others, he argued, act and react out of fear- the fear of being fired or reprimanded or of not being able to properly fulfill job responsibilities.

Perspective Three- Frederick Herzberg's Motivation-Hygiene Theory suggests that motivation is based on either satisfaction of dissatisfaction in the work place. These "hygiene" factors leading to satisfaction are achievement, recognition and advancement. Dissatisfaction factors are work conditions, monetary compensation and worker relationships. This theory suggests that supervisors must be able to manage these satisfaction and dissatisfaction factors in order to motivate employees. The key to motivating employees is to enrich their satisfaction.

Essay Task
Write a cohesive, logical essay considering multiple perspectives on what it is that motivates workers in the job place. In your essay, be sure to do the following:
· Analyze and evaluate the perspectives given

· State and develop your own perspective on the issue
· Explain the relationship between your perspective and those given

Note specifically what you are being asked to do. These pieces must be present in your essay. Your perspective may be in full or partial agreement or in total disagreement with those explored above. Whatever your perspective, be sure to support your ideas with logical reasoning and detailed, persuasive examples.

Planning & Writing Your Essay

As you think critically about the task and compose your essay, consider the following:

What are the strengths and weaknesses of the different perspectives on the issue?
· Identify the insights they present and what they fail to consider.
· Ascertain why a given perspective might persuade or fail to persuade.

How can you apply your own experience, knowledge, and values?
· Express your perspective on the issue, identifying the perspective's strengths and weaknesses.
· Formulate a plan to support your perspective in your essay.

Take 5
With time ticking away, it is hard not to jump in and immediately start writing, but stopping to think first is a crucial step. Taking 5 minutes to plan your essay out will save you the trouble of realizing you finally made it to your point after 35 minutes of writing, and it's too late to go back and revise.

Spend the first 5 minutes thinking about the issue, the perspectives, and your own views. What can you use as evidence? Is this issue like any other issue in terms of how it might be handled or mishandled? Is there anything in your own life that you can use as evidence? When it comes to the other perspectives, where do the arguments break down? Are there any logic problems? Do the perspectives work in some cases but not all? Answers to these questions give you an angle to start your writing, but it takes a few moments to think up some answers. So take them.

Make a Plan
If you like to write outlines, great. Write your thesis and jot down your ideas. If you don't, no problem; however, you still need to have your position and support set in your head. So write it down or don't, but make sure you have a good handle on what you're arguing and where you're headed with the essay.

Have a Few Templates in Mind
If writing leaves you frozen like a deer in the headlights, you might find it easier to have a few templates already in mind – roadmaps, if you will, that provide the overall structure. Your job is to fill in the places on the map where you're going to stop and ponder. Keep in mind, this is a basic framework. The more savvy you are with writing, the more you will move beyond this template. But for those of you who don't like the idea of timed writing, you will benefit from knowing you have a solid place to start the writing process.

Here's an example template.

Paragraph 1: Use an opening sentence to get the reader's attention. State your thesis. In a few more sentences briefly discuss your main points.

Paragraph 2: Use this paragraph to support your thesis. Have a topic sentence, an example, and a summary of the point. This paragraph is where you might introduce one of the perspectives that you agree with in whole or in part.

Paragraph 3: Use this paragraph to either bring up counter-arguments (think where your thesis disagrees with one or more of the perspectives) or to compare arguments (think where you thesis partially agrees with one or more of the perspectives). Use the same format as the previous paragraph – topic sentence, example, summary.

Paragraph 4: Use this paragraph as your conclusion. Restate your thesis, summarize your arguments, and present a strong ending. Don't be afraid to move beyond this basic form of conclusion – for example, present a what-if scenario or address another major counter-argument.

Pay Attention to the Particulars, but Don't Let Them

Overwhelm You
These essays are graded holistically. What that means is that the two people reading your essay are supposed to read them very quickly (in 3 minutes), focusing on what you did right, not what you did wrong.

Try to leave a minute or two to reread your essay at the end. Use the sub-vocalization technique. This means that you read as if you are reading out loud but very quietly. It's been proven that you will catch more errors by reading this way than simply reading with your eyes alone. Check for grammar problems, missing words, sentence fragments, and spelling errors.

Remember, you don't need to use big words to earn a high score. Sometimes trying to use words you don't normally use can work against you – you might spell them incorrectly or use them in the wrong context. No matter what, they will stick out and draw attention because they don't fit with the rest of the essay. Write cleanly, clearly, and coherently.

Take a Breath
Really, take a breath. This essay is more about quantity than quality. By quantity I don't mean the number of words, but rather the content. Do you provide an argument? Do you mention the three different perspectives? Do you offer concrete proof for your viewpoint (concrete means a solid example as opposed to a vague statement that something is true because you said so)? Do you have an introduction with a thesis, body paragraphs with evidence and explanation, and a conclusion?

Sounds a lot like the template above. Practice coming up with a few different templates to have at the ready, and you are already halfway there.

SCORING

To earn a high score on your essay, you must generate a sound perspective on the given issue (which brings the given perspectives into account) and then argue your perspective effectively. Essay readers/scorers are trained to evaluate the following:

Ideas and Analysis:
Your essay effectively produces relevant, sound ideas and engages fully with the perspectives given in the

prompt. It is clear that you understand the given issue, the purpose of your essay and the audience for whom you write.

Development and Support:
Your essay reflects your ability to explore ideas as you provide a solid rationale to enhance your argument. In this exploration of ideas, you are expected to fully explain, consider the implications and illustrate your thought process with examples. You must help your reader follow and understand your thoughts about the issue at hand.

Organization:
Your essay shows that as a writer you can organize your ideas clearly and with purpose. Because how you choose to organize your writing is an integral part of communicating effectively, you are expected to arrange your essay in a way that helps to carry the reader through your discussion by clearly indicating the relationship between ideas.

Language Use and Conventions:
Your essay should show that you have the ability to articulate a written argument clearly and with proper use of writing conventions: grammar, syntax, word usage and mechanics. It should also convey your awareness of your audience as you adjust the tone and style of your writing to communicate in an effective way.

Sample Responses and Scoring

Sample Response/Score of 1
I think people are motivated if their getting what they want. Like what the one guy says that if their satisfyed they'll work hard to get what they want and if your not happy you dont want to do nothing. My uncle bob hasnt worked for a long time cause he says his bosses dont ever appricate what he does anyhow so why bother. my teachers dont like how i act sometimes and they get really mean if i dont do my homework and if theyd chill out a little id probly work harder and like rite now im hungry when im hungry its hard to focus on my lesson when i didn't have brekfast or i staid up to late the nite before. So my perseptive is i think everybodys gotta get food and sleep to feel good enough to work and also like uncle bob need to be appricated.

Scoring Explanation
Ideas and Analysis = 1
There is no cohesive thesis that the essay works to support. Although the writer presents the idea that people are motivated to get what they want, the essay does not go on to fully support that idea. He then loosely brings in the idea of motivation based on the hierarchy of needs, but does not develop the idea or connect it with his opening statement. In essence, the essay seems to be a random collection of undeveloped, unrelated ideas.

Development and Support = 1
Although there is some development, the example of Uncle Bob and the writer's response to his teachers, the writer does not fully explore and explain his position.

Organization = 1
Again, there is some semblance of a central idea, but the writer does not build his argument in a logical, cohesive way. Instead he jumps back and forth between examples and perspectives with no transitions to smooth and unite the argument. There is no paragraphing or grouping of ideas.

Language Use = 1
This essay fails to exhibit much skill in language use. There are numerous errors in usage, mechanics, and punctuation, which inhibit the essay's clarity. Much of the word choice is simplistic and colloquial, which weakens the argument tremendously.

Sample Response/Score of 2
What motivates people to work hard? I think people work hard because of something they want. If someone wants something then they'll go for it.

Sometimes people work hard because their in need. If I need to fix my car well then I'll ask for more hours at my job. But they also might work hard just because that's what we're supposed to do. I work hard sometimes because my parents say I should. So if people have a need then they'll step up and do whatever they can to fill that need.

People also work hard to get a goal which is sort of like working for a need but maybe different. This is more like if they want a raise or a promotion of something like that. And in reverse they might work hard because their afraid they'll lose their job. So working because of fear or incentives may also be true.

Finally, I agree people work for satisfaction and dissatisfaction. I try to work hard on my school work because my parents want me to and I like to get as good of grades as I can. Bad grades mean I'm dissatisfied and I've let my parents down.

In conclusion, I agree with all the perspectives and think their all right in different ways. Basicly, I think its true that people work to get what they want.

Scoring Explanation

Ideas and Analysis = 2
This essay has a narrow scope with limited ideas presented. Although the writer attempts to address each of the given perspectives, there is little engagement of those perspectives with his own ideas. Instead, he simply states the given perspectives and attempts to give examples. Rather than building an argument, the analysis is loosely connected with the given perspectives, reflecting a weakness in both thought and purpose.

Development and Support = 2
Weak development fails to support and clarify this argument. The writer's initial statement that people work hard if they want something does not work sufficiently as a unifying thesis for the argument. In fact, the rest of the argument meanders off in different directions as the writer attempts to address each of the given perspectives. There is no real exploration or explanation of ideas, nor does the writer consider the implications of the perspectives within each paragraph. He then returns to his initial statement as he closes his essay with no final connection of his thought processes.

Organization = 2
Although the writer provides paragraphing in an attempt to structure his essay, the ideas are grouped with no clear connection. For example, the second paragraph suggests that people are motivated by need, but also includes the idea of being motivated by others' expectations. This idea is then repeated later in the essay as the writer discusses wanting to do well in school to please his parents. Although the writer uses transitions to begin each paragraph (also, finally, in conclusion), they do not effectively create a cohesive argument that builds from one idea to the next.

Language Use = 2
Awkward word choices throughout the essay impede understanding. (If I need to fix my car well then I'll ask for more hours. People...work hard to get a goal which I guess is sort of like working for a need but maybe different. Bad grades mean I'm dissatisfied...) There are a few other errors in spelling, punctuation and sentence structure that show a weakness in language use and weaken the overall argument.

Sample Response/Score of 3
People are motivated in different ways. Motivation is important and there are lots of different reasons why people want to do well. People are motivated in good ways and bad ways and that effects how they perform in their jobs and in school.

Some people are motivated because of their needs they don't have but they want. If someone has food and water, safety, and love, then having self-esteem can be something they work toward. If someone doesn't have self-esteem, then that becomes important to them. They will be motivated to do well in their job and earn praise and maybe even a raise so they can feel good about themselves.

In either work or in life, people can also be motivated by either incentives or fear. Some people want to achieve more money or more power or more respect. Others might work hard at their jobs or in school because they are afraid of being fired or getting in trouble in their classes. Either way, they work harder so that they can achieve more and so they won't have any negative consequences.

Lastly, people are motivated based on whether they are satisfied or dissatisfied. If they have achievement, recognition and advancement in their jobs, they are satisfied and will continue to work hard to keep these things because it makes them feel good and satisfied. If they don't like their jobs or aren't making a good salary or maybe don't like the people they work with then they are dissatisfied and won't work as hard. If their bosses know how they feel then they can maybe do things that will make them feel better, which will make them more satisfied and they will work harder.

In conclusion, people are motivated in different ways. They are motivated in good and bad ways and that effects how they do. It's important to understand how people are motivated so their bosses in charge of them can inspire them to achieve.

Scoring Explanation

Ideas and Analysis = 3

The writer clearly tried to generate a thesis. (People are motivated in good ways and bad ways and that effects how they perform in their jobs and in school.) However, the idea is very general. It gives the reader some sense of direction, but it sets the essay up for a simplistic analysis with no real exploration or debate. There is no engagement with the given perspectives. Rather the essay relies on repeating and agreeing with their claims. And although he tries to include examples- the idea that some people work not to be fired or not to get into trouble in classes, for instance- the analysis does not lend itself to an investigation of further implications and/or underlying assumptions.

Development and Support = 3

The essay presents a very general argument which is mirrored within the development of each paragraph. The writer does attempt to extend the argument with general examples within each paragraph, but these examples are not fully explained or explored. Had he in paragraph 3, for example, explored his example of fear being a strong motivator, his ideas might have had more strength and clarity. As written, the example requires the reader to make his own inferences of how and why fear (of losing one's job or getting in trouble in school) can be motivational. Also, rather than unique development, the essay is quite repetitive of the wording from the prompt.

Organization = 3

This essay is organized according to the traditional five-paragraph approach, which does bring a sense of organization to its ideas. Unfortunately, the writer has depended far too heavily on this structure which limits the essay's effectiveness. This traditional structure also limits any kind of meaningful connection from one topical paragraph to the next. This disconnect between paragraphs hinders any growing discussion and/or emergence of the writer's unique perspective on how and why people are motivated.

Language Use =3

Along with a few misused word forms and grammar errors (that effects how they perform, if someone doesn't have...it becomes important to them), the usage is simplistic. The ideas are clearly communicated, but the basic language does nothing to clarify or strengthen the argument. Occasional awkwardness in sentence structure (so their bosses in charge of them, their needs they don't have but want) show a limited level of skill in language use.

Sample Response/Score of 4

As more and more of society seems to be unmotivated, schools and employers have had to find ways to push people to do a good job. There are multiple theories of how to do that, and although motivating people is essential for schools and businesses to do, there is a question of how they can accomplish that goal. I believe that the best way to motivate others is by making them feel good about themselves, which can be done with incentives and with satisfaction.

The world has become a more complicated, perplexing place. People have to work harder than ever before to do well and to make a living, and that's because there is so much competition. In schools, students must work exceptionally hard to maintain a high grade point average and a high class rank. They are competing with all their classmates to have high scores. In their jobs, people have to toil endlessly and often endure long hours to make sure they are doing the very best job they can. Otherwise, there may be someone else standing in line to take their job away from them. If a worker cannot produce an acceptable amount of products on an assembly line, for example, he will lose his job to his competition. Therefore, he must be motivated.

Only when people feel good about themselves do they have the self-esteem needed to try to achieve. If someone doesn't like himself and doesn't feel worthy, he is less likely to feel like pushing himself toward a goal. However, individuals who have a high self-esteem feel as though they are worthy. That same worker will have confidence that he can not only meet but exceed the number of products he's expected to produce, and then he'll be able to do so.

Incentives can be motivational but fear is only a hindrance to motivation. Motivating with incentives is really just like motivating with self-esteem. When a person is rewarded for good performance, in school or at his job, he gains self-respect and confidence so he'll work even harder. He will want to feel even better about himself and want to keep receiving the incentives. In school, a student who gets an A feels good and wants to get more A's. Similarly, at work, a person who gets a raise feels good and wants to get another raise. Therefore, incentives lead to people to a higher self-esteem, which, in turn, creates both job satisfaction and future motivation.

Scoring Explanation

Ideas and Analysis = 4
The writer has a clear thesis that engages the three perspectives (self-esteem, incentives and satisfaction.) The writer then explores his thesis with examples and explanation (in school and in the workplace.) The writer also addresses the complexity of the issue. (Only when people feel good about themselves do they have the self-esteem needed to try to achieve. Incentives can be motivational but fear is only a hindrance to motivation.) Although the writer does not explicitly mention each perspective, it is clear that their ideas are support for his argument.

Development and Support = 4
The essay has clear lines of support that strengthen the thesis. The two main arguments are that students and workers must be motivated to achieve, and the writer carries his analysis forward by exploring why that motivation is essential. He gives a few solid examples- students competing for grades and class rank and workers competing to keep their jobs. The argument becomes one of what happens when these groups of people become unmotivated. And although the examples and discussion are there, they are somewhat limited. The writer also veers from the prompt each time he discusses motivation in schools as opposed to in business.

Organization = 4
The essay revolves around a clear organizational structure. The introduction identifies the thesis, which is centered on the three perspectives (feeling good about oneself, incentives and satisfaction.) The writer uses the second paragraph to begin to build an argument that motivation is important, setting the essay up to explore how best to achieve motivation in the following paragraphs. Paragraphs three and four

drive the argument forward with specific examples and discussion of the complicating evidence that fear is a hindrance to motivation. Transitions are used to connect ideas, most prevalently within the paragraphs (otherwise, therefore, similarly, however).

Language Use = 4
The writer has a firm grip on writing conventions and uses the language in a way that contributes to both the clarity and the overall effect of the essay. Strong word choices, such as perplexing, toil and endure emphasize the writers arguments without becoming redundant. There is a varied sentence style, which increases the readers' interest and creates a logic that helps to clarify and support the thesis.

Sample Response/Score of 5
Since the beginning of time as one person has attempted to influence another, the question of how to motivate another human being has puzzled mankind. Whether through making sure one's needs are met, through some system of rewards and punishments or through making sure an employee is happy on the job, most companies find themselves trying to determine exactly how it is they can motivate their workers. In reality, the answer to this age-old question may lie somewhere in the middle. We are all vastly different people and, therefore, how each of us is best motivated may be as individual as we are.

There is truth in Maslow's theory of the Hierarchy of Needs and many companies adhere to the theory that only when an employee has his basest needs met can he concern himself with any of the higher needs. If an employee, for example, is concerned about a loved one's health and safety, he most certainly will be focused on family rather than on his work. For this reason, some companies have instituted a Family Leave, allowing workers to take time off if they need to care for a family member. They understand that the employee will be more productive on the job if they can place their focus on their work as opposed to on their concern. Other companies have begun day care centers so working mothers will know their children are safe and well cared for while they are on the job. Still others have created a gym space within the company so employees can have a convenient place to work out and stay fit. With exercise and stress-relief readily available on the job site, workers are fulfilling lower needs. They can then relax and become more motivated to perform at their jobs.

There are some who argue that true motivation comes from what is called the "Carrot and Stick" theory, which purports that people are motivated either by incentives or by fear. This theory, however, is limiting as it does not take into account the complexity of human nature. It's true that sometimes fear can be motivating. Parents who punish their children by grounding them or taking away a prized possession align themselves with this theory. It's also true that sometimes the idea of a "reward" can be motivating. Parents who "pay for grades" abide by this theory. Although this can be successful in motivating children, it is much less successful in motivating employees. What this "Carrot and Stick" theory achieves instead of motivation is resentment. Adult workers expect to be treated as adults, not as children who need to be scolded for misbehaving. A company using this type of motivational approach may alienate those they are attempting to motivate.

While true motivation comes from an individual, innate sense of pride and quest to achieve, the idea that workers are motivated or not based on feelings of satisfaction or dissatisfaction is a blend of the other two theories. Workers who are satisfied in their work are not lacking in any of their base needs. They have food and shelter and love and, at least in part, a sense of self-esteem. If they were lacking in any of these, they would be dissatisfied and no amount of outside motivation would cure their discontent. Workers who are striving to achieve incentives do so to feel better about themselves and their work. They are rewarded by the reward and continue to work hard to benefit both monetarily and in terms of self-esteem.

Scoring Explanation
Ideas and Analysis = 5
This argument engages well with all the given perspectives. The writer sets forth his thesis, that motivation is as individual as we are, and is therefore able to present each perspective in an analysis that evaluates its usefulness in the workplace. Within this context, the writer addresses specifics of each perspective, along with relevant workplace examples. He addresses what he sees as a limitation to one of the perspectives, allowing it a modicum of truth but discerning its weaknesses. (This theory, however, is limiting as it does not take into account the complexity of human nature.) The writer is successful in a critical analysis as he drives his thesis toward a final conclusion, that the most useful perspective is a blend of the other two.

Development and Support = 5
The purpose of the essay is clear and the writer remains focused on this purpose throughout his argument. Each of the paragraphs and the sentences within work to enhance and support the thesis. The writer effectively reasons with specific examples and uses illustrations to clarify his argument that motivation comes in as many different packages as do individuals. He consistently helps the reader understand why the information he is presenting is important, as he does when he explains that workers whose base needs are met can relax and focus on their jobs and that using fear as a motivator in the workplace can lead to resentment. The writer also anticipates counter-arguments (It's true that fear is sometimes motivating), which allows him to further his analysis with his own counter that this type of motivation can lead to resentment. The thoughtful analysis creates a well-developed and compelling argument.

Organization =5
The organizational structure of this essay is cohesive and concise. The introduction presents a purpose-setting platform which engages the reader, (Since the beginning of time as one person has attempted to influence another, the question of how to motivate another human being has puzzled mankind.) The thesis, that successful motivation is different for each individual, allows the argument to test each of the given perspectives against relevant examples. There is also a solid logic in the essay's presentation, beginning with an analysis of the first and second perspectives, followed by a hypothesis that the third is a blend of the first two and, therefore, perhaps the most effective of the three. Traditional transitions (for example, while, however) are employed, as well as more sophisticated transitional phrasing (in reality, with exercise and stress-relief readily available) making a connection between and among the writer's thoughts and ensuring a smooth, enjoyable read.

Language Use =5
This essay employs many markers of advanced language use. Both the word choice and the sentence structure are varied and effective. The precise

language, including the strong verbs (puzzle, scold, align, adhere) concisely communicate the essay's ideas. The stylistic choices, such as the parallel use of "through" in the introduction (Whether through making sure one's needs are met, through some system of rewards and punishments or through making sure an employee is happy on the job), as well as the formal, academic tone that the writer adopts, demonstrate a strong understanding of both purpose and audience and work to advance the writer's intricate ideas.

Sample Response/Score of 6

In a society that is becoming more and more reliant on the government to support it, the question of how to motivate people in the workplace is more relevant than ever. Businesses need workers who are motivated to work hard. However, they often complain that workers no longer want to work, and they, unfortunately, don't seem to know what to do about it. If businesses want to succeed in today's complex marketplace, they must find new and innovative ways to motivate their workers.

Psychologists and philosophers have pondered the mystery of human motivation for hundreds of years, and each of the proposed theories has strengths and weaknesses. One of the most notable theories comes from Abraham Maslow with his theory of the Hierarchy of Needs. Maslow suggests that no one can be motivated to achieve beyond his present level of need. Someone who is hungry cannot be concerned with self-actualization. A worker, for example, who, for whatever reason, has no food in his pantry will be more concerned about his growling stomach than about whether or not he is voted most valuable employee. And while this is true, one does not necessarily follow the other. While someone who is hungry may not worry about achieving his full potential, someone who isn't hungry may be equally unconcerned about striving toward personal fulfillment through his job.

Equally limited is philosopher Jeremy Bentham's theory that individuals are motivated either through incentives or fear. If a business offers its workers incentives, either with over-time compensation or time off or any myriad of other incentives, those employees may or may not respond. There are plenty of people who want to put in their eight-hour work day and go home. They simply are not motivated to take on more work-related responsibilities than they have to to collect their paycheck at the end of each week, and no amount of money will change the fact that they want to live a simple existence with less stress and less time on the job. On the other hand, if workers are threatened, however subtly, in an attempt to instill fear, rather than being motivated, they are very likely to react with animosity. Rather than being inspired to work harder, those threatened with negative consequences will most likely become angry, disgruntled employees, which is detrimental to the working environment. In fact, such negativity can become infectious, destroying any positives the company may have going for it.

Less extreme than the other theories, Frederick Herzberg's Motivation-Hygiene theory purports that individuals are motivated based on their satisfaction at work. If those who work hard are rewarded with recognition and advancement- which is very similar to Bentham's incentive theory-Herzberg suggests they will be more motivated to achieve. This, however, has the same weakness as Bentham's theory. There are some who simply do not want to work hard. They are content to put in their time and collect their pay. Yes, these incentive-type theories, and even Maslow's theory of needs, will work for some. There are people who are driven to excel because they want to feel good about themselves. For these individuals who want to be recognized and rewarded for a job well-done, perhaps Maslow's theory comes closest to explaining the mysteries of motivation. The fact remains, however, that not all employees are created equally. There will always be individuals who are more concerned with their leisure time.

Ultimately, the theories run awry, and that is because how to motivate an individual must be based on his or her individual wants, needs and personality. Businesses cannot guarantee their employees motivation based on any one theory. Yes, rewards and incentives are an important part of any company's motivational policies. However, perhaps the most important part of any motivational strategy is to create an atmosphere of purpose and teamwork. When people feel that they have a purpose and that they belong- to a family or a group or even a job-based team- they are happier. When people are happy, they tend to have more energy and enthusiasm for their work. Perhaps this is, in part, what Maslow's hierarchy suggests. People need to be loved. They need to belong. If companies want to motivate all of their employees, they must create a strong, purposeful, caring atmosphere of which rewards are a part.

Scoring Explanation

Ideas and Analysis = 6

The argument establishes a framework in which the writer can effectively test the three given perspectives. The thesis, that businesses must find new and innovative ways to motivate employees, allows the writer to delve into the nuances of each perspective as he grows the argument into an examination of both strengths and weaknesses of each perspective. The thesis begins to evolve with a complication in the second paragraph (And while this is true, one doesn't necessarily follow the other) as the writer highlights a limitation of the first perspective. The writer then grows this complicating idea, that the perspectives must be critically examined for their logic, in the third paragraph as he explores the limitations of the second perspective. The writer delves into possible limitations of the third perspective in the fourth paragraph, and the thesis evolves again as he considers the success of Maslow's theory juxtaposed to the other two. Ultimately, this critical move sends the essay toward a satisfying end with a fully evolved thesis, that businesses "must create a strong, purposeful, caring atmosphere of which rewards are a part."

Development and Support = 6

An integrated logic and relevant illustrations successfully articulate the significance of this argument. The writer explores each of the perspectives in relation to what businesses should and should not do in their efforts to motivate workers. The writer uses hypothetical examples, such as some wanting to put in an eight-hour day and collect their pay and others wanting to live simply with fewer job responsibilities and less stress. Such illustrations concede the limitations of each of the perspectives and develop and support the thesis by highlighting weaknesses in company's motivational policies based on any of the given perspectives. The final body paragraph complicates the argument further by introducing the writer's own perspective, that teamwork must be a part of any motivational strategy.

Organization = 6

A consistent focus on examining the thesis drives this essay forward as the writer effectively complicates and evolves his argument. The writer skillfully shapes the argument, testing the perspectives against real-life, workplace illustrations. The essay progresses logically from the controlling idea that businesses must find innovative means of motivation to the limitations of the various motivational strategies to the final evolution that true motivation comes from a sense of belonging. The writer uses transitions effectively to reflect this organization (One does not necessarily follow the other; On the other hand, if workers are threatened; perhaps this is, in part, what Maslow's hierarchy suggests.) Transitions are also used effectively within the paragraphs (Equally limited, on the other hand, rather than being inspired, ultimately). The overall strategy of an evolving thesis supported by strong transitions strengthens the impact of the argument.

Language Use = 6

An exact vocabulary (reliant, innovative, disgruntled, infectious, awry) and a clear and varied sentence structure represent an advanced skill level of language use. There are no errors in mechanics or word use, which also reflects a precise skill level. Stylistic choices work to create an air of academic discourse (Yes, these theories, while this is true, perhaps this is in part, ultimately these theories run awry), which accentuates the writer's final call for a compromise, the blending of incentives and a caring atmosphere of belonging. As he concludes, the writer reverts to simple sentences with strong verbs (People need to be loved. They need to belong. Companies must), which strengthen his final call to action. These rhetorical strokes effectively clarify the thesis and enhance the argument in a persuasively stylistic way.

PRACTICE TEST 1

So, you think you're ready for Practice Test 1? Or maybe you just started, and you need to take the Pretest.

Either way, it's time to test what you know. Turn to the next page to begin.

Vocabulary

1 — Expansive most nearly means:
   A. Costly
   B. Vast
   C. Sensible
   D. Competitive

2 — Credible most nearly means:
   A. Enthusiastic
   B. Dishonest
   C. Reliable
   D. Professional

3 — Devastation most nearly means:
   A. Sadness
   B. Restoration
   C. Clarity
   D. Destruction

4 — Vague most nearly means:
   A. Unclear
   B. Specific
   C. Pessimistic
   D. Gloomy

5 — Irreverent most nearly means:
   A. Religious
   B. Disrespectful
   C. Humorous
   D. Boring

6 — Aversion most nearly means:
   A. Attraction
   B. Inclination
   C. Optimism
   D. Distaste

7 — Laborious most nearly means:
   A. Difficult
   B. Laid-back
   C. Noisy
   D. Lonely

8 — Interminable most nearly means:
   A. Dull
   B. Valuable
   C. Endless
   D. Rushed

9 — Achromatic most nearly means:
   A. Time-related
   B. Non-romantic
   C. Without color
   D. Before history

10 — Cursory most nearly means:
   A. Ungodly
   B. Rapid

C. Not smooth

D. In a circular motion

11 — Hearsay most nearly means:

A. Bovine

B. Secondhand information that can't be proven

C. Taking place in arid regions

D. Communicative

12 — Magnanimous most nearly means:

A. Latin

B. Large quantities of liquid

C. Forgiving

D. Antipasta

13 — Terrestrial most nearly means:

A. Of the earth

B. Ordinary

C. Something that exists in a "miniature" environment

D. Foreign

14 — Nonchalant most nearly means:

A. Magnanimous

B. Hurried

C. Indifferent

D. Positive

15 — Palpable most nearly means:

A. Tangible

B. Unconcerned

C. Capable of being manipulated

D. Easygoing

16 — Daub most nearly means:

A. Suave

B. Plaster

C. Heinous

D. Muddy

17 — Distend most nearly means:

A. Enforce

B. Soften

C. Swell

D. Indemnify

18 — Gaffe most nearly means:

A. Taciturn

B. Mistake

C. Fishlike

D. Cane

19 — Papal most nearly means:

A. Lightweight

B. Regal

C. Downtrodden

D. Leader of Catholicism

20 — Tarry most nearly means:

A. Delay

B. Black

C. Mossy

D. Cold

21 — Hoopla most nearly means:
   A. Cavernous
   B. Heinous
   C. Commotion
   D. Sweet

22 — Doctrinaire most nearly means:
   A. Negative
   B. Dogmatic
   C. Insipid
   D. Diffident

23 — Plumose most nearly means:
   A. Shy
   B. Sly
   C. Furry
   D. Feathery

24 — Supplant most nearly means:
   A. Amplify
   B. Clarify
   C. Uproot
   D. Stabilize

25 — Vagary most nearly means:
   A. Limitless
   B. Wispy
   C. Capable
   D. Caprice

26 — Calamari most nearly means:
   A. Shamu
   B. Digit
   C. Squid
   D. Matrimony

27 — Lethargic most nearly means:
   A. Apathetic
   B. Cozy
   C. Bouncy
   D. Deadly

28 — Teensy most nearly means:
   A. Adolescent
   B. Immature
   C. Tiny
   D. Feminine

29 — Bland most nearly means:
   A. Common
   B. Solid
   C. Rakish
   D. Dull

30 — Fulsome most nearly means:
   A. Cruel
   B. Copious
   C. Graceful
   D. Handy

31 — Nomenclature most nearly means:
   A. Jealousy
   B. Name
   C. Steadiness
   D. Aggression

32 — Reluctant most nearly means:
   A. Casual
   B. Timid
   C. Intense
   D. Unwilling

33 — Shabby most nearly means:
   A. Feline
   B. Horrid
   C. Despicable
   D. Miserly

34 — Alms most nearly means:
   A. Holiness
   B. Burn
   C. Charity
   D. Beverage

35 — Defer most nearly means:
   A. Remove
   B. Cancel
   C. Quiet
   D. Dela

Critical Reading

Passage 1:

"Concerning love, I had best be brief and say that when I read Bertrand Russell on this matter as an adolescent, and understood him to write with perfect gravity that a moment of such emotion was worth the whole of the rest of life, I devoutly hoped that this would be true in my own case. And so it has proved, and so to that extent I can regard the death that I otherwise rather resent as laughable and impotent."
[From Love, Poverty, and War by Christopher Hitchens]

1 — What is the main topic of this paragraph?
   A. Gravity
   B. Adolescence
   C. Death
   D. Love

2 — What is the speaker's main point about this topic?
   A. It is something to be resented
   B. It is something to laugh at
   C. It makes life worth living
   D. It is brief

3 — The final sentence is:
   A. The topic sentence
   B. The speaker's personal story that backs up his premise
   C. A detail sentence that contrasts the main topic to another equally major topic
   D. The beginning of a new topic not related to the first

4 — The antecedent of "it" in line 3 ("so it has proved") is:
   A. Moment
   B. Emotion
   C. Life
   D. Case

5 — The speaker views death as:
   A. Fearsome
   B. Powerless
   C. Inevitable
   D. None of the above

Passage 2:

"Silence is meaningful. You may imagine that silence says nothing. In fact, in any spoken communication, it plays a repertoire of roles. Just as, mathematically speaking, Earth should be called Sea, since most of the planet is covered in it, so conversation might be renamed silence, as it comprises 40 to 50 percent of an average utterance, excluding pauses for others to talk and the enveloping silence of those paying attention (or not, as the case may be.)"
[From The Art of Conversation: A Guided Tour of a Neglected Pleasure by Catherine Blyth]

6 — What is the main topic of the paragraph?
   A. Communication styles
   B. Paying attention
   C. Silence
   D. None of the above

7 — What is the main point of the paragraph?
   A. Silence is the main component of conversation, even though it is often overlooked
   B. Speaking less is preferred
   C. The Earth should be called the Sea because the Sea covers most of our planet
   D. Most people are not paying attention during conversations

8 — What is the purpose of comparing silence and conversation to Earth and Sea?
   A. To show how interdependent conversation and silence are
   B. To emphasize the importance that dialogue has in relationships across the world
   C. To provide a concrete example of the significant part that silence plays in conversations

D. To explain why people become more talkative near bodies of water

9 — What is the antecedent of the word "it" in line 3 ("covered in it")?
  A. Earth
  B. Sea
  C. Silence
  D. Planet

10 — In line 2, when it says that silence "plays a repertoire of roles," this is an example of what device?
  A. Alliteration
  B. Simile
  C. Personification
  D. A and C

Passage 3:
"Who can understand the clotted language of everyday American commerce: the memo, the corporation report, the business letter, the notice from the bank explaining its latest "simplified" statement? What member of an insurance or medical plan can decipher the brochure explaining his costs and benefits? What father or mother can put together a child's toy from the instructions on the box? Our national tendency is to inflate and thereby sound important. The airline pilot who announces that he is presently anticipating experiencing considerable precipitation wouldn't think of saying it may rain. The sentence is too simple – there must be something wrong with it." [From On Writing Well: The Classic Guide to Writing Nonfiction by William Zinsser]

11 — What is the main topic of the paragraph?
  A. "Clotted language"
  B. "American commerce"
  C. "Our national tendency"
  D. None of the above

12 — Which of the following is an example of what the speaker cites as "our national tendency" in our oral and written speech (line 5)?
  A. "The corporation report"
  B. "The child's toy"
  C. "The airline pilot"
  D. All of the above

13 — Which of the following does the speaker use to present his position?
  A. Hyperbole
  B. Metaphors
  C. Rhetorical questions
  D. All of the above

14 — What is the speaker's overall tone in this paragraph?
  A. Biting and accusatory
  B. Sarcastic and mocking
  C. Contemplative and didactic
  D. None of the above

15 — In line 2, why is the word "simplified" surrounded by quotation marks?
  A. To emphasize the simplicity of a bank statement
  B. To encourage the readers to contemplate the purpose of a bank statement
  C. To illustrate an example of an exception to the types of language the speaker has been discussing
  D. To indicate that the language of the bank statement is the opposite of the way in which it is described

Arithmetic Reasoning

1 — Emma borrowed a total of $1,200 with simple interest. She took the loan for as many years as the rate of interest. If she paid $432 in interest at the end of the loan period, what was the rate of simple interest on the loan?

    A. 5
    B. 15
    C. 9
    D. 6

2 — In mathematics class, you have taken five tests and your average test grade is 91%. On the next test, your grade is 78%. What is your new test average?

    A. 84.5
    B. 90.5
    C. 87.5
    D. 88.8

3 — Jorge and his younger sister Alicia have ages that combine to a total of 42. If their ages are separated by eight years, how old is Alicia?

    A. 25
    B. 32
    C. 17
    D. 11

4 — You are making a budget for your money very carefully. Buying a smoothie each day costs $3.59 during the week and $3.99 on weekends. How much does your weekly budget allow, if you have a smoothie each work day and one day on the weekend?

    A. $22.74
    B. $23.54
    C. $23.94
    D. $21.94

5 — Four out of twenty-eight students in your class must go to summer school. What is the ratio of the classmates who do not go to summer school in lowest terms?

    A. 6/7
    B. 1/7
    C. 4/7
    D. 3/7

6 — Gourmet cookies are regularly priced at 89 cents each. Approximately how much is each cookie if one and a half dozen sell for $12.89?

    A. 65 cents
    B. 82 cents
    C. 72 cents
    D. 80 cents

7 — Which of the following is not an integer?

    A. 0
    B. 1
    C. -45
    D. All of the answer choices are integers

8 — Subtracting a negative number is the same as adding a _____ number.

    A. Positive
    B. Negative
    C. Zero
    D. Irregular

9 — What are the factors of 128?

    A. 2
    B. 2, 64
    C. 2, 4, 8, 16

D. 1, 2, 4, 8, 16, 32, 64, 128

10 — What are the two even prime numbers?
    A. 0, 2
    B. -2, 2
    C. Cannot answer with the information given
    D. There is only one even prime number

11 — What are the prime factors of 128?
    A. 2
    B. 2, 3
    C. 2, 4, 8, 16, 32, 64
    D. Cannot answer with the information given

12 — What is the proper "name" for the following: $[(52 + 25) + 3] \div 58x$
    A. An equation
    B. An expression
    C. A polynomial
    D. An exponent

13 — What is the Greatest Common Factor (GCF) of 16 and 38?
    A. 2
    B. 16
    C. 19
    D. Cannot determine with the information given

14 — What is the Least Common Multiple (LCM) of 5 and 8?
    A. 13
    B. 40
    C. 80
    D. Cannot determine with the information given

15 — What is the value of 7! ?
    A. 127
    B. 3,490
    C. 5,040
    D. 12,340

16 — Which of the following is an irrational number?
    A. $\sqrt{4}$
    B. $\sqrt{9}$
    C. $\sqrt{17}$
    D. All of the above

17 — A "20% off" sale is on at the men's store. The new shirt that you want is priced at $27.95. Your final cost will include a 6% sales tax. How much will you pay for the shirt?
    A. $22.36
    B. $20.68
    C. $23.70
    D. $24.03

18 — Henrietta and her younger brother Henry have ages that combine to a total of 96. If their ages are separated by twelve years, how old is Henry?
    A. 38
    B. 40
    C. 42
    D. 44

19 — Subtracting a negative number results in what type of operation?
    A. Adding a positive number
    B. Adding a negative number

C. An irrational number
D. A prime number

20 — A coffee shop sells an average of 16 coffees per hour. The shop opens at 6:00 in the morning and closes at 5:30 in the afternoon. If each coffee costs $3.05, how much does the shop make in one day?

    A. $581.95
    B. $561.20
    C. $545.29
    D. $672.00

21 — At Wilson Elementary School, the sixth grade class includes 38 students in a class. Sixteen of the students are male. What percent of the class is female?

    A. 42%
    B. 58%
    C. 56%
    D. 62%

22 — What is the value of $x^{1/2}$?

    A. -x
    B. $\sqrt{x}$
    C. x^2
    D. 2x

23 — What is the Greatest Common Factor (GCF) of 15 and 36?

    A. 2
    B. 3
    C. 4
    D. 5

24 — What the relationship between 240 and 2?

    A. =
    B. >
    C. <
    D. None of the above

25 — What is the value of f ? $f = (2^{-2} * 8) \div (0.5 * 4)$

    A. $\sqrt{2}$
    B. 1
    C. 4
    D. Cannot determine with the information given

26 — The Ice Cream Shoppe sells an average of 70 ice cream cones per hour. The shop opens at 10:30 in the morning and closes at 11:30 in the evening. If half of the ice cream cones sold cost $3.00 and half of the ice cream cones sold cost $4.50, how much does The Ice Cream Shoppe make in one day?

    A. $840.00
    B. $1,255.50
    C. $2,420.75
    D. $3,412.50

27 — Which of the following is an integer?

    A. 9.75
    B. 5 1/2
    C. $\sqrt{2}$
    D. 21

28 — What are the prime factors of 14?

    A. 1, 14
    B. 1, 2, 7, 14
    C. 1, 2, 3, 5, 7, 11, 14
    D. None of the above

29 — At Walla Wall High School, there are a total of 857 students. Twenty four of the students are in the TAG program. Half of the students in the TAG program are male. Eighty per cent of the seniors in the TAG program have been accepted at Ivy League universities. What percent of the student body is NOT in the TAG program?

A. 88%
B. 92.3%
C. 97.2%
D. 99.3%

30 — You are now "on your own", and have decided to create a basic budget to track your income and expenses. Buying a coffee at Starbucks each day during weekdays costs your $3.89. On the weekends, you indulge yourself with a $6.20 super smoothie at a health store both days. How much will your weekly "drink allowance" cost you per year?

A. $834.50
B. $852.20
C. $1,656.20
D. $4,190.00

31 — Write the $\sqrt{63}$ in simplest form.

A. $3\sqrt{7}$
B. $\sqrt{9} * \sqrt{7}$
C. $7\sqrt{9}$
D. $7\sqrt{3}$

32 — Write the $\sqrt{(45 / 7)}$ in simplest form.

A. $3\sqrt{7}$
B. $\sqrt{9} * \sqrt{7}$
C. $3/7\ \sqrt{35}$
D. $7\sqrt{3}$

33 — The decimal value for $\sqrt{78}$ lies between which integer pair?

A. 6 and 7
B. 7 and 8
C. 8 and 9
D. 9 and 10

34 — Write the $\sqrt{(72s^3b^7)}$ in simplest form.

A. $6bs\sqrt{2sb^6}$
B. $6bs\sqrt{2s^2}\ b^3$
C. $6b^2s\sqrt{2sb^3}$
D. $6b^3s\sqrt{(2sb)}$

35 — The decimal value of 7/11 is _____?

A. 1.57
B. 0.70
C. 0.6363…
D. 0.77

36 — The decimal value of 5/8 is _____?

A. 0.625
B. 0.650
C. 0.635
D. 0.580

37 — The fractional value of 0.5625 is _____?

A. 7/15
B. 11/23
C. 5/8
D. 9/16

38 — The fractional value of 0.3125 is _____?

A. 5/16
B. 4/24

C. 6/19

D. 9/25

39 — Express 17/10,000 in scientific notation.

A. $17 * 10^{-3}$

B. $17 * 10^{-4}$

C. $1.7 * 10^{-3}$

D. $1.7 * 10^{-4}$

40 — Express 736.589 in scientific notation.

A. $7.36589 * 10^{-3}$

B. $7.36589 * 10^{-2}$

C. $7.36589 * 10^{3}$

D. $7.36589 * 10^{2}$

Mathematics Knowledge

1 — If x = 15, find the value of f in the following equation: $f = (x^2/3) - 8$
    A. 67
    B. 667
    C. 57
    D. 83

2 — What does 638,000 signify in scientific notation?
    A. 6.38 * 1000
    B. $6.38 * 10^5$
    C. $6.38 * 10^{-5}$
    D. 638 * 1000

3 — Solve the following ratio: 11! / 8! [note: this ratio could also be expressed like this: 11! : 8!]
    A. (11/8)!
    B. 1.375
    C. 990
    D. 12.5

4 — What is the value of 8^3?
    A. 64
    B. 48
    C. 24
    D. 512

5 — Solve for the unknown variable P: P = (Q + 7) (Q + 3)
    A. 2Q+10
    B. $Q^2 + 10Q + 21$
    C. $Q^2 + 4Q + 21$
    D. $Q^2 + 4Q + 10$

6 — Place the following fractions in order from largest to smallest: 3/5, 1/4, 3/8, 5/9.
    A. ¼, 3/8, 3/5, 5/9
    B. 5/9, 3/8, 3/5, ¼
    C. ¼, 3/5, 3/8, 5/9
    D. 3/5, 5/9, 3/8, ¼

7 — What is the mode of the following sequence of numbers? 2, 3, 3, 5, 5, 5, 7, 7, 8, 10, 10, 12
    A. 3
    B. 5
    C. 10
    D. 12

8 — If a kid's toy rocket is designed to shoot half-a-mile into the air, but it only goes up 70% of that height, how many yards in altitude did the toy rocket reach?
    A. 422
    B. 610
    C. 616
    D. 921

9 — If y = 4, given the following equation, what is the value of x? x = (2y - 5) ÷ 2
    A. 0.2
    B. 1.5
    C. 39
    D. 40

10 — Solve the following ratio and express it in simplest form: 36:4!
    A. 1:1
    B. 1.5:1

C. 3.5:1
D. 64:1

---

1 — What percentage of 20 is 15?
   A. 15%
   B. 20%
   C. 50%
   D. 75%

---

2 — 12 is 15% of some number. What is 20% of that same number?
   A. 8
   B. 12
   C. 16
   D. 24

---

3 — If x = 3, find the value of f in the following equation: $f = (x^2/3) - 3$
   A. -3
   B. 0
   C. 3
   D. 6

---

14 — What is the mode of the following sequence of numbers?
       2, 3, 3, 3, 5, 5, 7, 7, 8, 10, 10, 12, 12, 13, 13, 14, 14, 15, 15
   A. 3
   B. 5
   C. 10
   D. 12

---

15 — What is the value of 13^3?
   A. 160
   B. 170
   C. 176
   D. 2,197

---

16 — Assume that X is 60% of Y, and Y is 80% of Z. If Z is 40, what is the value of X?
   A. 4.8
   B. 19.2
   C. 20.4
   D. 22.6

---

17 — Place the following fractions in order from largest to smallest: 2/5, 1/3, 3/7, 5/8.
   A. 5/8, 2/5, 3/7, 1/3
   B. 1/3, 2/5, 3/7, 5/8
   C. 5/8, 3/7, 2/5, 1/3
   D. Cannot determine with the information given

---

18 — A brown bag contains 4 yellow, 3 violet, and 4 black balls. All of the balls are of different sizes. Two balls are chosen from the bag. How many combinations can result in the selection of at least 1 yellow ball?
   A. 12
   B. 34
   C. 48
   D. 64

---

19 — If x and y are natural numbers, what are the possible solutions for x and y for the following equation:
       $3x + 2y = 11$
   A. (1,4)
   B. (4,1)
   C. (3, 1) and (4,1)
   D. (1,4) and (3,1)

---

20 — What is the average weight of the group of watermelons (listed below) that were delivered to Joe's Corner Store, and how much should Joe pay if he is paying $0.32/pound?

Watermelon weight: 6, 7, 7, 9, 12, 12, 15, 23, 23
      A. 11.46 pounds; $32.45
      B. 12.67 pounds; $36.48
      C. 16.73 pounds; $45.22
      D. 26.80 pounds; $45.22

21 — Is the value of Y a prime number, assuming A = 2? $Y = [(A^3 + A) \div 2] - 2$
      A. Yes
      B. No
      C. Cannot determine from the information given
      D. No, but the value of Y is a polynomial

22 — Solve the following equation for R, assuming that ß = 36 and μ = 144: $R = (\sqrt{ß} * \sqrt{μ}) \div (ß - μ)$
      A. -0.67
      B. 1.56
      C. 1.94
      D. Cannot determine with the information provided

23 — What is the average weight of the group of apples shown below that were delivered to Jack's Deli, and how much should Jack pay if he is paying $0.86/pound?   Apple weight: 6, 7, 7, 7.5, 8, 8, 9.5, 11, 11
      A. 5.54 pounds; $62.45
      B. 8.33 pounds; $64.50
      C. 11.3 pounds; $75.25
      D. 16.9 pounds; $88.50

24 — Solve the following equation to determine the value of Z: $Z = (R + 5)(R + 30)$
      A. $R^2 + 35R + 35$
      B. $R + 35R + 150$
      C. $R^2 + 35R + 150$
      D. $R^4 + 35R^2 + 150$

25 — If NASA produced a rocket booster that is designed to launch three-and-a-half miles into the air before dropping away into the ocean below, but it only went up 92% of that desired height, how many feet in altitude did the rocket booster reach, rounded to the nearest ten feet?
      A. 14,224
      B. 14,380
      C. 17,000
      D. 23,560

26 — Evaluate the expression $7x^2 + 9x - 18$ for x = 7.
      A. 516
      B. 424
      C. 388
      D. 255

27 — Evaluate the expression $x^2 + 7x - 18$ for x = 5.
      A. 56
      B. 42
      C. 38
      D. 25

28 — Evaluate the expression $7x^2 + 63x$ for x = 27.
      A. 5603
      B. 4278
      C. 6804
      D. 6525

29 — Simplify the expression $35a^4b^3c^2 + 65a^6b^7c^4$.

    A. $5a^4b^3c^2 (7 + 13a^2b^4c^2)$

    B. $5 (7a^4b^3c^2 + 13a^6b^7c^4)$

    C. $5b^3 (7a^4c^2 + 13a^6b^4c^4)$

    D. $5b^3a^4 (7c^2 + 13a^2b^4c^4)$

30 — Multiply the binomials $(x+3) (x-7)$.

    A. $x^2 - 4x + 21$

    B. $x^2 + 4x + 21$

    C. $x^2 + 4x + 21$

    D. $x^2 - 4x - 21$

Vocabulary

1 — B. Vast
Rationale: Expansive means covering a wide area regarding space or scope; extensive; wide-ranging.

2 — C. Reliable
Rationale: Credible means able to be believed; convincing; plausible; tenable.

3 — D. Destruction
Rationale: Devastation means great destruction or damage; ruin, havoc, wreckage.

4 — A. Unclear
Rationale: Vague means of uncertain, indefinite, or unclear character or meaning; indistinct; ill-defined.

5 — B. Disrespectful
Rationale: Irreverent means showing a lack of respect for people or things that are generally taken seriously; disdainful; scornful; derisive; contemptuous.

6 — D. Distaste
Rationale: Aversion means a strong dislike or disinclination; abhorrence; antipathy.

7 — A. Difficult
Rationale: Laborious means a task, process, or journey requiring considerable effort or time; arduous; strenuous.

8 — C. Endless
Rationale: Interminable means unending; monotonously or annoyingly protracted or continued; unceasing; incessant.

9 — C. Without color
Rationale: Achromatic means free from color.

10 — B. Rapid
Rationale: Cursory means hasty and therefore not thorough or detailed; perfunctory; desultory; casual; superficial.

11 — B. Secondhand information that can't be proven
Rationale: Hearsay means information received from other people that one cannot adequately substantiate; rumor; gossip.

12 — C. Forgiving
Rationale: Magnanimous means very generous or forgiving, especially toward a rival or someone less powerful than oneself; generous; charitable; benevolent.

13 — A. Of the earth
Rationale: Terrestrial means of, on, or relating to the earth.

14 — C. Indifferent
Rationale: Nonchalant means having an air of indifference or easy concern.

15 — A. Tangible
Rationale: Palpable means capable of being touched or felt; tangible.

16 — B. Plaster
Rationale: Daub means plaster; to cover or coat with soft adhesive matter; to apply crudely.

17 — C. Swell
Rationale: Distend means to enlarge from internal pressure; to swell; to become expanded.

18 — B. Mistake
Rationale: Gaffe means a social or diplomatic blunder; mistake; faux pas.

19 — D. Leader of Catholicism
Rationale: Papal means of or relating to a pope or the Roman Catholic Church.

20 — A. Delay
Rationale: Tarry means to delay or be tardy in acting or doing; to linger in expectation; wait.

21 — C. Commotion
Rationale: Hoopla means a noisy commotion; boisterous merrymaking.

22 — B. Dogmatic
Rationale: Doctrinaire means very strict in applying beliefs and principles; dogmatic; dictatorial.

23 — D. Feathery
Rationale: Plumose means having feathers or plumes; feathered.

24 — C. Uproot
Rationale: Supplant means to supersede another, especially by force or treachery; uproot; to eradicate and supply a substitute for; to take the place of and serve as a substitute, especially because of superior excellence or power; replace.

25 — D. Caprice
Rationale: Vagary means an erratic, unpredictable, or extravagant manifestation, action, or notice; caprice.

26 — C. Squid
Rationale: Calamari means squid used as food; the inky substance the squid secretes.

27 — A. Apathetic
Rationale: Lethargic means indifferent; apathetic; sluggish.

28 — C. Tiny
Rationale: Teensy means tiny.

29 — D. Dull
Rationale: Bland means smooth and soothing in manner or quality; exhibiting no personal concern or embarrassment; unperturbed; not irritating, stimulating, or invigorating; soothing; dull; insipid; stories with little plot or action.

30 — B. Copious
Rationale: Fulsome means characterized by abundance; copious.

31 — B. Name
Rationale: Nomenclature means name, designation; a system of terms used in a particular science, discipline, or art.

32 — D. Unwilling
Rationale: Reluctant means holding back; averse; unwilling; disinclined.

33 — C. Despicable
Rationale: Despicable means mean; despicable; contemptible; clothed with worn or seedy garments; threadbare and faded with wear; ill-kept; dilapidated.

34 — C. Charity
Rationale: Alms means something (as money or food) given freely to relieve the poor; charity.

35 — D. Delay
Rationale: Defer means to put off; delay; postpone; suspend.

Critical Reading

1 — D. Love
Rationale: "Concerning love . . . " — the speaker's first words, which provide a useful clue as to what the rest of the paragraph will be about

2 — C. It makes life worth living
Rationale: Hitchens says, in mid-paragraph, ". . . a moment of such emotion [love] was worth the whole of the rest of life."

3 — C. A detail sentence that contrasts the main topic to another equally major topic
Rationale: In the final sentence, the speaker compares his knowledge of love to his knowledge of death and declares that the depth of love that he has experienced has caused him to lose his resentment toward death.

4 — A. Moment
Rationale: What ("it") has been proven in the speaker's own life is that a "moment of such an emotion" of love was worth the whole rest of his life."

5 — B. Powerless
Rationale: The speaker's experience of love has rendered death as weak, or lacking in power.

6 — C. Silence
Rationale: The main topic of the passage is silence; the first sentence states that silence is meaningful, and the rest of the passage goes on to support that claim.

7 — A. Silence is the main component of conversation, even though it is often overlooked
Rationale: Most communication is non-verbal. It can take the form of bodily gestures, facial expressions, body language, etc., but it can also be in the form of the silence that exists between utterances.

8 — C. To provide a concrete example of the significant part that silence plays in conversations
Rationale: The Earth/Sea comparison is an analogy to illustrate the great percentage of conversation that is comprised of silence.

9 — B. Sea
Rationale: The planet, despite being called, Earth, is mostly covered in Sea ("it").

10 — D. A and C
Rationale: Discussing silence as "playing roles" is an example of personification, or giving human qualities to an inanimate or abstract object. "Repertoire of roles" is an example of alliteration, where the "r" sound is repeated in close succession within the line.

11 — A. "Clotted language"
Rationale: The speaker's main topic is that of the "clotted language" used by most of the nation. According to the speaker, we tend to use too many and too complex words when fewer, simpler ones will do.

12 — A. "The corporation report"
Rationale: The corporation report is the only form of speech, or language, that is a problem because it has become our "national tendency." It is a written document comprised of text, i.e. language. The airline pilot uses language, but he himself is not an example of language. Neither is the child's toy, though its instructions use language.

13 — C. Rhetorical questions
Rationale: The speaker uses several rhetorical questions to encourage his readers to consider the overuse of inflated language that has become ubiquitous in our daily lives; other than citing specific examples of where such language can be found (like a business letter or list of insurance benefits) and asking rhetorical questions, the speaker does not use any other literary devices to present his point.

14 — B. Sarcastic and mocking
Rationale: The speaker is clearly making fun of our tendency to inflate our language, especially when quoting the lengthy announcement from the pilot and then "translating" it into simple English. The "simplified" bank statement is an example of his saying the opposite of what he means. And in his final sentence—"The sentence is too simple – there must be something wrong with it" —it is clear that the speaker is being tongue-in-cheek about this national phenomenon.

15 — D. To indicate that the language of the bank statement is the opposite of the way in which it is described

Rationale: The paragraph's main point is that we tend to overinflate our language in written and oral forms. The bank statement is one example of this, so when the speaker puts quotation marks around the word simplified, he is quoting the language of the bank while simultaneously mocking them because his point is that the statement is anything but simple.

Arithmetic Reasoning

1 — D. 6
The correct answer is D. Rationale: The loan was for $1,200, and the amount paid out was $432. You know that the number of years of the loan and the interest rate of the loan is the same number.

There are the four possible scenarios in the multiple choice answers:

5 — 5 years * 0.05 = 0.25 * 1,200 = $300 paid in interest
15 — 15 years * 0.15 = 2.25 * 1,200 = $2,700 paid in interest
9 — 9 years * 0.09 = 0.81 * 1,200 = $972 paid in interest
6 — 6 years * 0.06 = 0.36 * 1,200 = $432 paid in interest

This method of finding the correct answer is based on eliminating the incorrect ones as much as finding the correct one. Often the time spent trying to find an equation or formula is more than the time needed to just model the possible outcomes.

2 — D. 88.8
The correct answer is D. Rationale: If you have taken 5 tests and your average grade was 91% (0.91), then you have earned a total of 455 points out of a possible 500 points thus far; 5 * 0.91 = 4.55. If you have earned a grade of 78% on the next test, you must have gotten 78 points out of a possible 100 points which can be added to the previous total points for your grade

Therefore, you have earned 455 + 78 = 533 out of a possible 600 points. Since you have taken 6 tests, divide the number of points earned by the number of tests you have taken:

553/600 = 0.8883 or 88.83%.

3 — C. 17
The correct answer is C. Rationale: Rather than try figure out a proper formula, ask yourself, "What if Jorge and Alicia were the same age? If their combined ages are 42, then they would each be 21 years old. Since they are 8 years apart, Jorge has to "get older" by 4 years and Alicia has to "get younger" by 4 years. Therefore, add 4 years to Jorge to get 25 years of age, and subtract 4 years from Alicia to get 17 years of age. It might be good to check your results before basking in the glory of knowing how to do this problem! If Jorge + Alicia should equal 42, then 25 + 17 = 42. Check! Remember, the question is asking about Alicia's age, not Jorge's.

4 — D. $21.94
The correct answer is D. Rationale: In this scenario, you will be buying a smoothie each day during the workweek — five times — and once on the weekend. The weekend smoothie will cost slightly more. Notice that you will NOT be buying a smoothie on one of the two weekend days. The weekly cost of your smoothie consumption (SC) can be determined in the following manner:

SC = (3.59 * 5) + (3.99 * 1)
SC = 17.95 + 3.99
SC = 21.94

5 — A. 6/7
The correct answer is A. Rationale: If 4 out of 28 students ARE going to summer school, then 24 out of the 28 student ARE NOT going to summer school. Therefore, to find out the ratio, you divide 24 by 28, and then simplify your fraction by dividing both the numerator and the denominator by 4, which is the same thing as multiplying the fraction by 1 because 4/4th = 1:

24/28 = (24 ÷ 4)/(28 ÷ 4) = 6/7

6 — C. 72 cents
The correct answer is C. Rationale: Reading the question carefully, you will note that the regular price for the cookies is irrelevant since the question is only about the price for each cookie if you buy one and a half dozen, i.e. 18, cookies. If 18 cookies cost $12.89, then 1 cookie costs 12.89/18 = 0.716, or $0.716, and rounded up they each cost $0.72 or 72 cents.

7 — D. All of the answer choices are integers
The correct answer is D. Rationale: An integer is defined as a number that can be written without a fraction or decimal component. The set of integers includes zero (0), the natural numbers (1, 2, 3 . . .), also called whole numbers or counting numbers. It also includes their additive

inverses, the negative integers (-1, -2, -3 . . .).

8 — A. Positive

The correct answer is A. Rationale: Within an equation, subtracting a negative number (-A), will give the same result as adding the corresponding positive number (A). Here's an example:

Z + Y = Z - (-Y)
43 + 6 = 43 - (-6)

9 — D. 1, 2, 4, 8, 16, 32, 64, 128

The correct answer is D. Rationale: Factors are the set of numbers that can be multiplied to form a given number. 128 is created in the following ways:

128 = 2 * 64
128 = 4 * 32
128 = 8 * 16
128 = 1 * 128

Therefore, factors of 128 are simply the set of these factors: 1, 2, 4, 8, 16, 32, 64, 128

10 — D. There is only one even prime number

The correct answer is D. Rationale: By definition, there is only one even prime number; 2. Memorize it. Prime numbers are natural numbers greater than 1 that have no positive divisors other than 1 and itself. A composite number is a natural number greater than 1 that is not a prime number. For example, 7 is prime because no integer (natural number), other than 1 and itself, can be divided into it without remainder. The even number 10, for example, is a composite number because both 2 and 5 can be divided into it without remainder.

11 — A. 2

The correct answer is A. Rationale: The prime factorization of 128 is found in the following way:

128 = 2 * 64 = 2 * 2 * 32 = 2 * 2 * 2 * 16 = 2 * 2 * 2 * 2 * 8 = 2 * 2 * 2 * 2 * 2 * 4

The prime factorization of 128 is the last form in the above list. The question asked what the prime factors of 128 are. In the final form two is the only number in the prime factorization of 128.

12 — B. An expression

The correct answer is B. Rationale: By definition, an equation is a statement that two mathematical expressions are equal. Notice that an equation has, by definition, an equal sign. A polynomial is an expression of more than two algebraic terms, especially terms that contain different powers of the same variables. Notice that a polynomial is a specific type of expression. An exponent is a quantity representing the power to which a given number or expression is to be raised. The exponent is the superscript symbol beside the number or expression. There is no exponent in the given quantity.

Since none of these mathematic terms can be used to describe the given information, it must be an expression. An expression is a collection of symbols that jointly express a quantity.

13 — A. 2

The correct answer is A. Rationale: The Greatest Common Factor (GCF) is found by identifying all of the factors of the two or more numbers in your set, and then finding the largest number that they share.

Factors of 16 are 1, 2, 4, 8, 16
Factors of 38 are 1, 2, 19, 38

The greatest (largest) common factor these two numbers share is 2.

14 — B. 40

The correct answer is B. Rationale: The Least Common Multiple (LCM) is found by listing numbers that are integer multiples of the original number. Multiplying a given number by all of the integers (1, 2, 3, 4, 5, 6 etc.):

For the number 5 — 5, 10, 15, 20, 25, 30, 35, 40, 45, 50, etc.
For the number 8 — 8, 16, 24, 32, 40, 48, 56, 64, etc.

The LCM is the smallest number that appears in both sets of multiples; in this case the number 40.

15 — C. 5,040

The correct answer is C. Rationale: The use of the exclamation sign with a number simply means that the number is multiplied by all of the integers smaller than that number. In this example:

7! = 1 * 2 * 3 * 4 * 5 * 6 * 7 = 5,040

16 — C. √17

The correct answer is C. Rationale: If a square root is not expressed as an integer, it is an irrational number. Since √4 = 2 and √9 = 3, they are not irrational numbers. However, √17 cannot be expressed as an integer because it is irrational. The most notable irrational number is probably "pi", which is very useful in geometry; it is equal to approximately 3.14159. It is important to note that this is an approximate value.

17 — C. $23.70

The correct answer is C. Rationale: To pay for the shirt, you will pay 20% less because of the sale and 6% more because of the tax; however, it is important to note that you will only pay 6% on the sale price. Therefore, first calculate the sale price:

$27.95 * 0.80 = $22.36

Now, calculate the price of the sales tax:

$22.36 * 0.06 = $1.34

Finally, add the sale price and the sales tax:

$22.36 + $1.34 = $23.70

18 — C. 42

The correct answer is C. Rationale: If Henry and his sister were the same age (for example, if they were twins), and their combined age was 96, they would both be 48 (96 divided by 2). However, if their ages are 12 years apart, Henrietta's age needs to be increased by 6 years, and Henry's needs to be decreased by 6 years. Since the question is asking only about Henry's age, simply subtract 6 years from the average age of 48 to find that the correct answer is 42 years old.

As a check, Henrietta's age should be 48 + 6 or 54 years old. Their combined ages, therefore, would be 42 + 54 = 96 years, the given part of the problem.

19 — A. Adding a positive number

The correct answer is A. Rationale: Subtracting a negative number, is the same as adding a positive number. Another way to think of it is to think, in simple terms, that "two negatives make a positive."

20 — B. $561.20

The correct answer is B. Rationale: If the shop opens at 6:00am and closes at 5:30pm, it is open a total of 11.5 hours. Selling 16 coffees/hour, they sell (11.5 * 16) or 184 coffees/day. Each coffee costs $3.05, so in one day they will take in (184 * 3.05) or $561.20.

21 — B. 58%

The correct answer is B. Rationale: First, ignore that it is the 6th grade class — that number is perhaps included to distract you. If there are 16 males, there must be 22 female students. If you are looking for the percentage of female students, you divide the number of female students by the total number of students (22 ÷ 38) or 0.5789 or 57.89%. Rounding up to 58% is correct, since all the answer choices are whole numbers.

22 — B. √x

The correct answer is B. Rationale: A fractional exponent is equivalent to the root of the number. If the exponent is 1/2, it is equivalent to the square root. If the exponent is 1/3, it is equivalent to the cube root. The word "square" is used because squaring the square root returns the number inside the root; the word "cube" is used because cubing the cube root returns the number inside the root.

23 — B. 3

The correct answer is B. Rationale: The Greatest Common Factor (GCF) is found by identifying all of the factors of the two or more numbers in your set, and then finding the largest number that they share.

Factors of 15 = 1, 3, 5, 15
Factors of 36 = 1, 2, 3, 4, 9, 12, 18, 36

The greatest (largest) common factor these two numbers share is 3.

24 — C. <

The correct answer is C. Rationale: Any integer with zero as its exponent equals one. So, the question is asking, "Is one equal to, greater than, or less than two", or "none of the above." This should be an easy choice. It may help if you remember that the arrow points to the smaller number. So 1 < 2.

25 — B. 1

The correct answer is B. Rationale: The formula is:

$f = (2^{-2} * 8) \div (0.5 * 4)$

A number with a negative exponent is the "fraction" or reciprocal of its value. So, if $2^2 = 4$:

$2^{-2} = 1/4 = 0.25$ and
$f = (0.25 * 8) \div (0.5 * 4)$
$f = 2 \div 2$
$f = 1$

26 — D. $3,412.50

The correct answer is D. Rationale: First, notice that if half the ice cream cones cost $3.00 and half of them cost $4.50, then the average of all of the ice cream cones sold will be $3.75. Next, notice that the store is open for 13 hours each day. If The Ice Cream Shoppe sells, on average, 70 cones per hour, than you need to calculate how many cones they sell in one day:

13 * 70 = 910 ice cream cones sold in one day

Now you can calculate how much money the store takes in during an average day:

910 * $3.75 = $3,412.50

27 — D. 21

The correct answer is D. Rationale: An integer is a number that can be written as a whole number (without a fractional or decimal component). The set of integers consists of zero, the whole/counting/natural numbers (1, 2, 3, ...), and the additive inverses of those numbers (-1, -2, -3, ...).

28 — D. None of the above

The correct answer is D. Rationale: Prime factors of a positive integer are the prime numbers that divide into that integer exactly. Since 1 and the integer given do not "divide" the number, they are not included in the list of prime factors for a given number. Therefore, the prime factors of 14 are 2 and 7; a choice not listed as one of the answers.

29 — C. 97.2%

The correct answer is C. Rationale: After reading the question and specifically what the question is asking — the "percent of the student body that is NOT in the TAG program" — you should first notice that there is extraneous information. The fact that 50% of the students in the TAG program are male, and the fact that 80% of the seniors in the TAG program have been accepted at Ivy League universities, are both irrelevant and are intended to distract you. If you read the question carefully, you will realize that it is fairly simple. In this example, one of the important numbers is in word form:

24/857 = 0.028 = 2.8%

So, 2.8% of the students ARE in the TAG program. Notice, however, that they are asking you what percentage are NOT in the TAG program:

100% - 2.8% = 97.2%

30 — C. $1,656.20

The correct answer is C. Rationale: To calculate your weekly drink expenses (WDE), knowing there are 5 weekdays (Monday-Friday) and 2 weekend days (Saturday and Sunday):

WDE = (3.89 * 5) + (6.20 * 2)
WDE = 19.45 + 12.40
WDE = 31.82

However, the question asks you for your yearly drink expenses, and there are 52 weeks in a year:

$31.82/week * 52 weeks/year = $1,656.20

Wow! When you look at it this way, that's a lot of money for a drink each day! If you could manage not to have that habit, but instead put that money under your mattress for 30 years, you'd have almost $50,000 saved!

31 — A. $3\sqrt{7}$

The correct answer is A. Rationale – $\sqrt{63}$ can be rewritten as the product of two radicals, $\sqrt{9} * \sqrt{7}$. The part of that product that can be expressed as an integer is $\sqrt{9}$, which is 3. In simplified form, the square root can be written as $3\sqrt{7}$.

32 — C. $3/7 \sqrt{35}$

The correct answer is C. Rationale – $\sqrt{(45 / 7)}$ can be rewritten as the ratio of two radicals, $\sqrt{45} / \sqrt{7}$, but mathematical conventions do not allow a radical in the denominator. To "rationalize" that ratio, both the numerator and denominator must be multiplied by $\sqrt{7}$. In a simplified form, the ratio can be written as $(\sqrt{45} * \sqrt{7}) / 7$. This can still be simplified because $\sqrt{45}$ can be written as the product of $\sqrt{9} * \sqrt{5}$. The part of that product that can be expressed as an integer is $\sqrt{9}$, which is equal to 3. Therefore, since $\sqrt{5} * \sqrt{7}$ equals $\sqrt{35}$, in final simplified form, the ratio becomes $3/7 \sqrt{35}$.

33 — C. 8 and 9

The correct answer is C. Rationale – The perfect squares are as follows:

$6^2 = 36$
$7^2 = 49$
$8^2 = 64$
$9^2 = 81$
$10^2 = 100$

Since 78 is between 64 and 81, the $\sqrt{78}$ lies between 8 and 9.

34 — D. $6b^3s\sqrt{(2sb)}$

The correct answer is D. Rationale – $\sqrt{(72s^3b^7)}$ can be rewritten as the product of three radicals: $\sqrt{72} * \sqrt{s^3} * \sqrt{b^7}$. This method allows the solution to focus on one factor at a time. The numerical part of that square root product, which can be expressed as a product of two square roots, is $\sqrt{72} = \sqrt{36} * \sqrt{2}$. Since the $\sqrt{36}$ equals 6, the numerical part of the solution is $6\sqrt{2}$. The factor $\sqrt{s^3}$ can be written as $\sqrt{s^2} * \sqrt{s^1}$, which simplifies to $s\sqrt{s}$. Finally, $\sqrt{b^7}$ can be written as $\sqrt{b^6} * \sqrt{b^1}$, which simplifies to $b^3\sqrt{b}$. In simplified form, the square root $\sqrt{(72s^3b^7)}$ can be written as the product of all three parts, i.e. $6b^3s\sqrt{(2sb)}$.

35 — C. 0.6363…

The correct answer is C. Rationale – The ratio 7/11 implies division, so the decimal value can be determined by the long division problem of 7 divided by 11. The long division results in the repeating decimal 0.6363… However, there is another method that may be simpler. The ratio 7/11 is the product of 7 times 1/11. The ratio 1/11 is the repeating decimal 0.0909…, so multiplying that decimal by 7 is 0.6363…, which is the same answer. If this method seems easier or faster, remember that every fraction with 11 in the denominator can be determined in the same way.

36 — A. 0.625

The correct answer is A. Rationale – The ratio implies division, so 5/8 can be determined by the long division problem of 5 divided by 8. The long division results in the decimal 0.625. However, there is a method to find this decimal that may be simpler. The ratio 5/8 is the product of 5 times 1/8. The ratio 1/8 is the decimal 0.125, so multiplying that decimal by 5 is 0.625, which is the same answer. If this method seems easier or faster, remember that every fraction with 8 in the denominator can be determined in the same way.

37 — D. 9/16

The correct answer is D. Rationale – The numerator in the correct ratio will be equal to the given decimal times the correct denominator. It is simply a result of cross-multiplying. But first, these problems can be greatly simplified if you eliminate incorrect answers.

For example, answers A and B can both be eliminated because they are both less than 0.5 or 1/2. If you can't see that, then multiply 0.5 times

5 and 0.5 times 23. In answer A, 0.5 times 15 is 7.5, so 7/15 is less than the fractional value of 0.5625. In answer B, 0.5 times 23 is 11.5, so 1/23 is less than the fractional value of 0.5625.

Now, evaluating fractional answers this way, you may look at answer C and realize that 0.6 times 8 equals 4.8. Since 4.8 is less than the numerator and 0.6 is larger than the given decimal value, C can be eliminated. The correct answer is D.

---

38 — A. 5/16

The correct answer is A. Rationale – The numerator in the correct ratio will be equal to the given decimal times the correct denominator. It is simply a result of cross-multiplying. But first, these problems can be greatly simplified if you eliminate incorrect answers.

For example, answer B can be eliminated because it can be simplified to 1/6, which is much less than 0.3125. If you can't see that, then divide 1 by 6, which equals 0.167.

For answer D, the ratio 9/25 is a simplified form of 36/100 or 0.36. This value is greater than the given decimal of 0.3125, so answer D can be eliminated.

Now, evaluating fractional answers this way, you may eliminate answer C for a very simple reason. 19 times 0.3125 will always leave a value of 5 in the ten-thousandths place because 19 times 5 equals 95. That means the product can never be the whole number 6, so answer C can be eliminated.

The correct answer is A because you have logically eliminated all the other possible choices.

---

39 — C. 1.7 * 10⁻³

The correct answer is C. Rationale – The ratio 17/10,000 implies division, which is 0.0017. These ratio conversions are simpler if the correct description is used for 17/10,000. In other words, the ratio is "seventeen ten thousandths" or 0.0017. The scientific notation must begin with 1.7, and since the decimal place will be moved three places to the right, the correct value is $1.7 * 10^{-3}$.

---

40 — D. 7.36589 * 10²

The correct answer is D. Rationale – The number 736.589 conversion to scientific notation starts with the decimal expression 7.36589. Since the decimal place was moved two places to the left, the correct value is $7.36589 * 10^{2}$.

Mathematics Knowledge

1 — A. 67
The correct answer is A. Rationale: Substituting 15 for x in the equation, it becomes: f = (15²/3) - 8

Since 15² = 225

f = 225/3 - 8
f = 75 - 8
f = 67

2 — B. 6.38 * 10⁵
The correct answer is B. Rationale: Scientific notation is a way to simplify large numbers by writing the number into a number that is one or more but not up to ten, followed by ten to the nth power. Here's an example that helps illustrate this concept:

123,456 = 1.23456 * 105

If the decimal place in 1.23456 is then moved over 5 places, you will get the original number — 123,456.

In the same way, 638,000 can be simplified into scientific notation by shifting the decimal place over 5 places:
638,000 = 6.38 * 105

Answer choices A and D cannot be correct because they do not include an exponent to indicate the "power of 10". Answer choice C would lead to a very small number instead of a large one since any number with a negative exponent becomes one divided by the number with a positive exponent.

3 — C. 990
The correct answer is C. Rationale: A number followed by an exclamation mark has a value found by multiplying all of the counting numbers beginning with one and ending with that specific number. In this example, you would find the following values for the two given numbers:

11! = 1 * 2 * 3 * 4 * 5 * 6 * 7 * 8 * 9 * 10 * 11
8! = 1 * 2 * 3 * 4 * 5 * 6 * 7 * 8

You could find the value of each of these numbers:

11! = 39,916,800
8! = 40,320

The ratio would be found simply by dividing these two numbers: 39,916,800/40,320 = 990. Therefore, the ratio would be 990:1.

There is a less "laborious" way to find this result. If you are dividing these two numbers, they share share all the terms between 1 and 8; therefore, those terms can be factored out, leaving only the following:

9 * 10 * 11 = 990

4 — D. 512
The correct answer is D. Rationale: You can answer correctly easily when you observe that 8³ = 8 * 8 * 8 = 64 * 8 = 512. Remember that another way to write this is the following: 8³ = 8² * 8¹ = 64 * 8.

5 — B. Q² + 10Q + 21
The correct answer is B. Rationale: This is an example of polynomial multiplication. When you recognize a formula in this form, you need to do the following:

1. Multiply the first term in each set of parentheses: Q * Q = Q²
2. Add the product of the first and last terms in each set of parentheses: 7Q + 3Q = 10Q
3. Multiply the second terms in each set of parentheses: 7 * 3 = 21

If you now put these three results in the same expression, you get the following:

P = Q² + 10Q + 21

Here's an example with the assumption that Q = 3:

P = (Q + 7) (Q + 3)
P = (3 + 7) (3 + 3)
P = 10 * 6
P = 60

Now, you want to substitute Q = 3 into the formula developed:
P = Q² + 10Q + 21
P = 3² + (10)(3) + 21
P = 9 + 30 + 21
P = 60

The numerical example of the equation checks out correctly!

---

6 — D. 3/5, 5/9, 3/8, ¼
The correct answer is D. Rationale: This question can be answered converting each fraction into its decimal equivalent:

3/5 = 0.6
1/4 = 0.25
3/8 = 0.375
5/9 = 0.555
The decimal equivalents, from largest to smallest, would be 0.6, 0.555, 0.375, 0.25.

Therefore, the fractions, from largest to smallest, would be 3/5, 5/9, 3/8, 1/4.

---

7 — B. 5
The correct answer is B. Rationale: The "mode" in a set of data is simply the one item that occurs most often; in this question, the number 5 repeats itself 3 times, more than any other number.

---

8 — C. 616
The correct answer is C. Rationale: Two conversion factors will be required: one mile = 5,280 feet and one yard = 3 feet.

The rocket is designed to go to a height of 5,280 feet ÷ 2 or 2,640 feet. Because it only reaches 70% of its designed altitude, the rocket achieved an altitude of 2,640 feet * 0.7 or 1,848 feet. To convert this into yards, divide by 3: 1,848 feet ÷ 3 feet/yard or 616 yards.

---

9 — B. 1.5
The correct answer is B. Rationale: Substitute the value of y into the given equation:

x = (2y - 5) ÷ 2
x = [(2 * 4) - 5] ÷ 2
x = (8 - 5) ÷ 2
x = 3 ÷ 2
x = 1.5

---

10 — B. 1.5:1
The correct answer is B. Rationale: The key here is to find the value of 4! The value of a number ending with an exclamation is that number multiplied by all the other whole numbers less than that number; for example:

4! = 4 * 3 * 2 * 1
4! = 24

Now substitute this number into the given ratio and simplify it:
36:24 or 1.5:1

11 — D. 75%

The correct answer is D. Rationale: A percentage problem is a simple ratio. The expression "what percentage of 20" can be designated as the unknown variable x. "Percentage" means a value divided by 100. The expression "of," implies multiplication. The expression "is 15" just means = 15. So, to find the percentage of 20 that is 15:

x = 15 ÷ 20 = 0.75
x = 0.75 * 100 = 75%

To change a decimal into a percentage, simply multiply by 100.

12 — C. 16

The correct answer is C. Rationale: The first step is to write an equation to solve for "some number":

"12 is 15% of some number" translates to x = 12 ÷ 0.15 = 80

However, the question is asking for 20% of that number, 80. To find 20% of 80, multiply by the decimal equivalent of 20%, or 0.2; this then translates to y = 80 * 0.2 = 16.

13 — B. 0

The correct answer is B. Rationale: If you substitute 3 for x in the equation, you get the following:

f = (3²/3) - 3

Since 3² = 9
f = 9/3 - 3
f = 3 - 3
f = 0

14 — A. 3

The correct answer is A. Rationale: The "mode" in a set of data is simply the one that occurs most often; in this question, the number 3 repeats itself 3 times, more than any other number.

15 — D. 2,197

The correct answer is D. Rationale: You can easily answer this correctly when you observe that 13³ = 13 * 13 * 13 = 169 * 13 = 2,197. Remember that another way to write this is the following: 13³ = 13² * 13¹ = 169 * 13

The values for answer choices A, B. and C are all close to 169 or 13², and the value of 13² still has to be multiplied by another 13!

16 — B. 19.2

The correct answer is B. Rationale: To solve this problem, first write out what you know:

X = 60% of Y
Y = 80% of Z
Z = 40

You can substitute the value of Z into the second equation, remembering that you can always convert a percentage into a decimal by dividing by 100:

Y = 80% * 40 = 0.8 * 40 = 32

Now, in a similar operation, substitute the value of Y into the first equation:

X = 60% * 32 = 0.6 * 32 = 19.2

17 — C. 5/8, 3/7, 2/5, 1/3

The correct answer is C. Rationale: This question can be answered in several ways, but perhaps the easiest is to convert each fraction into its decimal equivalent:

$/5 = 0.4$

$/3 = 0.33$

$/7 = 0.429$

$/8 = 0.625$

he order of the decimal equivalents, from largest to smallest, would be the following:

.625, 0.429, 0.4, 0.33

herefore, the order of the fractions, from largest to smallest, would be the following:

/8, 3/7, 2/5, 1/3

t should have been easy to put 5/8 first on the list because it was the only one greater than 1/2.

---

8 — B. 34

he correct answer is B. Rationale: First, consider the scenario with one yellow ball and one non-yellow ball being selected. Since there are yellow balls, there is a 4:11 chance that one yellow ball will be chosen. Since there are 7 balls that are either violet or black, there is a 7:11 hance that a ball of another color will be chosen. Therefore, there will be 28 (4 * 11) combinations that allow both a yellow ball and a ball f another color to be chosen. There are 110 (11 * 10) total combinations.

Next, consider the possibility that both of the balls chosen are yellow. If these 4 balls are labeled as Y1, Y2, Y3, and Y4, next determine how nany combinations there can be.

f Y1 is chosen, its "partner" can be Y2, Y3, or Y4   (3 possible choices)

f Y2 is chosen, its "partner can be Y3 or Y4   (2 possible choices)

f Y3 is chosen, its "partner" can be Y4   (1 possible choice)

To summarize:

Y1 + Y2

Y1 + Y3

Y1 + Y4

Y2 + Y3

Y2 + Y4

Y3 + Y4

Since there are 28 combinations involving one yellow ball and 6 combinations involving two yellow balls, there are 34 combinations that allow at least one yellow ball to be chosen.

---

19 — D. (1,4) and (3,1)

The correct answer is D. Rationale: The natural numbers are the whole positive numbers beginning with 1. Also, notice from the answer choices that the only possible answers include the numbers 1, 3, and 4, and any equations that have 2 as either x or y should not be considered.

If x = 1

3x + 2y = 11

(3 * 1) + 2y = 11

3 + 2y = 11

2y = 8

y = 4

Therefore, one possible pair of natural numbers are x = 1 and y = 4.

Remember, x = 2 should not be considered. If x = 2 then y = 5/2. It must be an integer

If x = 3

3x + 2y = 11

(3 * 3) + 2y = 11

9 + 2y = 11
2y = 2
y = 1

Therefore, another possible pair of natural numbers are x = 3 and y = 1.

If x = 4
3x + 2y = 11
(3 * 4) + 2y = 11
12 + 2y = 11
2y = -1
y = -1/2

Because -1/2 is not a natural number, this pair of numbers should not be considered.

20 — B. 12.67 pounds; $36.48

The correct answer is B. Rationale: You calculate the average weight by adding the weights of all the watermelons delivered and dividing that total by the number of watermelons delivered.

watermelon-weightavg = (6 + 7 + 7 + 9 + 12 + 12 + 15 + 23 + 23) ÷ 9
watermelon-weightavg = 114 ÷ 9
watermelon-weightavg = 12.67 pounds

If Joe is paying $0.32/pound for 114 pounds of watermelons, he will have to pay the following amount:
114 pounds * $0.32/pound = $36.48

21 — A. Yes

The correct answer is A. Rationale: Substitute the value of A into the given equation:

Y = [(A3 + A) ÷ 2] - 2
Y = [(23 + 2) ÷ 2] - 2
Y = [(8 + 2) ÷ 2] - 2
Y = (10 ÷ 2) - 2
Y = 5 - 2
Y = 3 (a prime number)

22 — A. -0.67

The correct answer is A. Rationale: Substitute the values you know:

If ß = 36, then √36 = 6
If μ = 144, then √144 = 12

Now you can insert those values into the given equation:

R = (√ß * √μ) ÷ (ß - μ)
R = (6 * 12) ÷ (36 - 144)
R = 72 ÷ -108
R = -0.67

Sometimes these problems might look difficult because the Greek letters represent the variables. The Greek letters are no different than the x's and y's that we normally use.

23 — B. 8.33 pounds; $64.50

The correct answer is B. Rationale: You calculate the average weight by adding the weights of all the apples delivered and dividing that total by the number of apples delivered.

apple-weightavg = (6 + 7 + 7 + 7.5 + 8 + 8 + 9.5 + 11 + 11) ÷ 9
apple-weightavg = 75 ÷ 9

apple-weightavg = 8.33 pounds

If Jack is paying $0.86/pound for 75 pounds of apples, he will pay $64.50.

24 — C. $R^2 + 35R + 150$

The correct answer is C. Rationale: This is an example of polynomial multiplication. When you recognize a formula in this form, remember that this type of formula can always be solved in this manner:

$(P + 3) (P + 7) = P^2 + (3+7)P + (3 * 7)$

To check to see if this formulation works, assume P = 4

$(P + 3) (P + 7) = P^2 + 10P + 21$
$(4 + 3) (4 + 7) = 4^2 + [(10)(4)] + 21$
$7 * 11 = 16 + 40 + 21$
$77 = 16 + 40 + 21$
$77 = 77$

Okay, the equivalence works! Now, apply the method to this question:

To check your answer, assume that R = 2:

$(R + 5)(R + 30) = R^2 + 35R + 150$
$(2 + 5)(2 + 30) = 2^2 + [(35 * 2)] + 150$
$7 * 32 = 4 + 70 + 150$
$224 = 224$

25 — C. 17,000

The correct answer is C. Rationale: To solve this problem, we will use the following conversion of units:

one mile = 5,280 feet

This is because the given units are in miles but the answer units are in feet. The rocket booster is designed to go up three and a half miles:

5,280 feet * 3.5 = 18,480 feet

Because it only reaches 92% of its designed altitude, the maximum becomes:

18,480 feet * 0.92 = 17,001 feet.

Rounded to the nearest ten feet, the correct answer is:

17,000 feet

26 — C. 388

The correct answer is C. Rationale – The value can be expanded as 7 * 49 added to 9 * 7, with 18 subtracted from the total. That becomes 343 + 63 -18, with the answer equal to 388.

27 — B. 42

The correct answer is B. Rationale – The value can be expanded as 25 added to 5 * 7, with 18 subtracted from the total. That becomes 25 + 35 -18, with the answer equal to 42. There is another simple way to evaluate this expression. The expression can be rewritten as the product of two expressions (x+9)(x-2). If you substitute 5 for x, then this product becomes 14 * 3, which is also 42.

28 — C. 6804

The correct answer is C. Rationale – The simplest way to evaluate this expression is to rewrite it as the product of two expressions. Factoring common factors out, the given expression becomes 7x(x+9). "7x" becomes 189 and x+9 becomes 36. The product of 189 and 36 becomes 6804. In the interest of eliminating incorrect answers, the product of the values in the "ones" column is 6 * 9, which is 54. The correct answer must end in 4, so the correct answer must be C.

29 — A. $5a^4b^3c^2 (7 + 13a^2b^4c^2)$

The correct answer is A. Rationale – The best way to simplify an expression such as this is to identify term by term the greatest common factors (GCF). In the integer coefficients, the GCF of 35 and 65 is 5. The numerical coefficients inside the parentheses become 7 and 13. Similarly, the GCF of a^4 and a^6 is a^4. The other two GCF factors are b^3 and c^2. Factoring common factors outside of the parentheses leaves the expression $7 + 13a^2b^4c^2$ inside the parentheses.

30 — D. $x^2 - 4x - 21$

The correct answer is D. Rationale – Multiplying the two binomials together with FOIL means that the first term is the product of the two x's, or x^2. However, the last term is the product of 3 and -7, which means that answer D is the only correct answer. The middle term is the sum of 3x and -7x, which is -4x. Again, answer D is the only correct answer. If you choose to use the box method to solve these products, you will see the same results and the same factors.

ACCUPLACER - Spire Study System

PRACTICE TEST 2

Round 2. You've been studying with Spire for about a month — you're almost done!

Turn to the next page to begin.

Vocabulary

1 — Macerate most nearly means:
    A. Accelerate
    B. Lauding
    C. Yearn
    D. Soften

2 — Pouch most nearly means:
    A. Hit
    B. Level
    C. Bag
    D. Terror

3 — Tenet most nearly means:
    A. Renter
    B. Belief
    C. Spy
    D. Numerical

4 — Transverse most nearly means:
    A. Corrupt
    B. Rapid
    C. Against
    D. Across

5 — Bounteous most nearly means:
    A. Hilly
    B. Polite
    C. Giving
    D. Conservative

6 — Sheath most nearly means:
    A. Remove
    B. Handle
    C. Cut
    D. Case

7 — Doodad most nearly means:
    A. Filial
    B. Husband
    C. Gadget
    D. Keepsake

8 — Grandiose most nearly means:
    A. Motherly
    B. Miserly
    C. Handy
    D. Grand

9 — Pastiche most nearly means:
    A. Hodgepodge
    B. Stickiness
    C. Cartoon
    D. Journal

10 — Replica most nearly means:
    A. Copy
    B. Vegetable
    C. Dinosaur

D. Tool

11 — Screwball most nearly means:
A. Hurried
B. Saucy
C. Zany
D. Timorous

12 — Dictum most nearly means:
A. Correction
B. Erasure
C. Pronouncement
D. Assembly

13 — Formulate most nearly means:
A. Experiment
B. Devise
C. Foster
D. Terrorize

14 — Jolly most nearly means:
A. High
B. Jovial
C. Weak
D. Constipate

15 — Peptic most nearly means:
A. Active
B. Vigilant
C. Concerned
D. Digestive

16 — Shrill most nearly means:
A. Terrestrial
B. Intemperate
C. Howling
D. Cursory

17 — Collude most nearly means:
A. Infiltrate
B. Plot
C. Align
D. Portray

18 — Entreat most nearly means:
A. Enjoy
B. Consign
C. Fulminate
D. Plead

19 — Melodramatic most nearly means:
A. Harmful
B. Catchy
C. Sensational
D. Oblivious

20 — Primal most nearly means:
A. Modern
B. Divisible
C. Primitive
D. Accountable

21 — Slack most nearly means:
  A. Moist
  B. Negligent
  C. Topping
  D. Silken

22 — Thwart most nearly means:
  A. Toad
  B. Hurry
  C. Cannibalize
  D. Contravene

23 — Grudge most nearly means:
  A. Stereotype
  B. Malice
  C. Dirty
  D. Delicious

24 — Kinetic most nearly means:
  A. Sly
  B. Monotonous
  C. Dynamic
  D. Afloat

25 — Parrot most nearly means:
  A. Overhead
  B. Colorful
  C. Dominating
  D. Repeat

26 — Rivulet most nearly means:
  A. Liquid
  B. Squishy
  C. Brook
  D. Allowance

27 — Souse most nearly means:
  A. French
  B. Immerse
  C. Question
  D. Terrify

28 — Buttress most nearly means:
  A. Spread
  B. Canonize
  C. Dunk
  D. Support

29 — Callous most nearly means:
  A. Scarred
  B. Unfeeling
  C. Hard
  D. French

30 — Impetuous most nearly means:
  A. Impulsive
  B. Preventative
  C. Royal
  D. Repulsive

31 — Vehemently most nearly means:
  A. Widely
  B. Wisely
  C. Intensely
  D. Intentionally

32 — Elucidate most nearly means:
  A. Confuse
  B. Explain
  C. Monitor
  D. Greek

33 — Guile most nearly means:
  A. Deceit
  B. Intention
  C. Strategy
  D. Care

34 — Commodious most nearly means:
  A. Imperial
  B. Dirty
  C. Roomy
  D. Loaded

35 — Engender most nearly means:
  A. Cause
  B. Sexualize
  C. Endanger
  D. Stupefy

Critical Reading

Passage 1:

"When someone works for less pay than she can live on – when, for example, she goes hungry so that you can eat more cheaply and conveniently – then she has made a great sacrifice for you, she has even made you a gift of some part of her abilities, her health, her life. The "working poor", as they are approvingly termed, are in fact, the major philanthropists of our society. They neglect their own children so that the children of others will be cared for; they live in substandard housing so that other homes will be shiny and perfect; they endure privation so that inflation will be low and stock prices high. To be a member of the working poor is to be an anonymous donor, a nameless benefactor, to everyone else." [From Nickel and Dimed: On Not Getting By in America by Barbara Ehrenreich]

1 — What is the main topic of this paragraph?
   A. Job variety
   B. Philanthropy
   C. The working poor
   D. The talents and skills needed to procure work

2 — What techniques does the speaker use to develop her ideas?
   A. Definition
   B. Compare and contrast
   C. Emotional appeals
   D. All of the above

3 — What is the speaker's overall tone in this paragraph?
   A. Formal and critical
   B. Blunt and sympathetic
   C. Harsh and sarcastic
   D. Ambivalent and introspective

4 — Why are the words "working poor" surrounded by quotation marks the first time they are seen in this paragraph (line 3)?
   A. To emphasize that it is an oxymoron
   B. Because it is a term she has coined for a group she has observed
   C. Because it is a formal term to describe a common group found in society today
   D. To mock a phrase that is chronically used incorrectly

5 — With which of the following statements about the working poor would the speaker agree?
   A. They are lazy
   B. They are neglectful parents
   C. They are integral to the smooth-functioning of society
   D. They make the lives of the wealthy simpler and more enjoyable

Passage 2:

"Take a moment to imagine what it would be like to live robustly to a ripe old age of one hundred or more. Then, as if your master switch clicked off, your body just goes kaput. You die peacefully in your sleep after your last dance that evening. You don't die of any particular illness, and you haven't gradually been wasting away under the spell of some awful, enfeebling disease that began years or decades earlier. Most of us can't picture ourselves avoiding the ailments that tend to end others' lives prematurely and sometimes suddenly. Yet I want you to believe that you can live a long, fulfilling, disease-free life – because it is possible. The end of illness is closer than you think. It is my wish for you. But to achieve this superhuman feat, you have to understand health from a new perspective and embrace a few tenets of well-being that probably go against everything you've ever learned." [From The End of Illness by David B. Agus]

6 — What is the speaker's main point in this paragraph?
   A. We must relearn the ways to achieve good health
   B. Illness is responsible for all premature death
   C. Illness is possible to avoid
   D. We can all live to be over one hundred years old

7 — The speaker uses the second person pronoun to achieve what effect?
   A. An informal style
   B. A direct address
   C. A lecturing tone

D. Both A and B

8 — Which technique does the speaker use to establish his point?
  A. Process analysis
  B. Cause and effect
  C. Hypotheticals
  D. None of the above

9 — What is the antecedent of "it" in line 7?
  A. "Life"
  B. "End of illness"
  C. "Feat"
  D. "Spell"

10 — What is the speaker's overall tone in the paragraph?
  A. Contemplative
  B. Didactic
  C. Doubtful
  D. Morose

Passage 3:

"I do not argue categorically against assimilation. Such an argument would be rash, for assimilation is often a precondition of civilization – to speak a language, to curb violent urges, and to obey the law are all acts of assimilation. Through such acts we rise above the narrow stations of our lives to enter into a broader mindfulness, and often, paradoxically, we must do this to elaborate ourselves as individuals. I argue here only against coerced assimilation not supported by reasons – against a reflexive conformity that takes itself as its own rationale. What will constitute a good enough reason for assimilation will be controversial, and I am for the most part encouraging us to have that conversation rather than seeking to impose my own canon. But one illegitimate reason is simple animus against a particular group – the demand that gays assimilate to straight norms, or that women assimilate to male norms, or that racial minorities assimilate to white norms – because one group is considered less worthy than another." [From Covering: The Hidden Assault on Our Civil Rights by Kenji Yoshino]

11 — With which of the following statements would the speaker NOT agree?
  A. Assimilation is a necessity of an ordered society
  B. Assimilation helps us develop our personal identities
  C. Assimilation helps us determine which groups are less worthy than others
  D. The reasons for assimilation must be determined jointly by all members of society

12 — What is the speaker's overall tone in this passage?
  A. Critical
  B. Self-effacing
  C. Satirical
  D. None of the above

13 — What is the paradox to which the speaker refers in line 4?
  A. Minorities will never be accepted into mainstream society
  B. Civilization dictates that all members of society be assimilated
  C. Everyone realizes the need for assimilation, but no one wants to engage in formal conversation about it
  D. Assimilation forces us to be both self-aware and aware of others simultaneously

14 — Which adjective best describes the speaker's writing style?
  A. Formal
  B. Grandiloquent
  C. Colloquial
  D. Lyrical

15 — According to the speaker's definition, what would be an example of "coerced assimilation" (line 5)?
  A. Requiring that all men keep their hair cut short
  B. The societal segregation of blacks and whites
  C. Making it illegal for women to leave the house without their heads covered
  D. None of the above

Arithmetic Reasoning

— What is the relationship between 1000 and 1?
   A. =
   B. >
   C. <
   D. None of the above

— Assume that X is 250% of Y, and Y is half of Q. If Q is 4.5, what is the value of X?
   A. 6.25
   B. 5.625
   C. 9.25
   D. Cannot determine from the information provided

— 861 is 20% of what number?
   A. 0.0023
   B. 172.2
   C. 4,305
   D. Unable to determine from the information given

— What percentage of 20 is 15?
   A. 15%
   B. 20%
   C. 70%
   D. 75%

— What mathematical property is exemplified in the following formula? $x(y + z) = xy + xz$
   A. Associative Property
   B. Commutative Property of Sums
   C. Distributive Property
   D. Newton's Three Laws

— What would be the likely next number in the following pattern?   2, 5, 10, 17, 26, ?
   A. 32
   B. 34
   C. 37
   D. 41

— What mathematical property is exemplified in the following formula? $a(yz) = (ay)z$
   A. Associative Property of Multiplication
   B. Associative Property of Addition and Multiplication
   C. Commutative Property of Sums
   D. None of the above

— What is the absolute value of - 4.7?
   A. 4.5
   B. 0
   C. 4.7
   D. 20.68

— What is the reciprocal of ß?
   A. 1 ÷ ß
   B. ß$^{-1}$
   C. 1/ß
   D. All of the above

10 — In mathematics class, you have taken 5 tests and your average test grade is 91%. Your next test grade is a 78%. What is your new test average?
   A. 84.5%
   B. 90.5%

C. 87.5%
D. 88.8%

11 — At Wilson Elementary School, the sixth grade class includes 38 students. Sixteen of the 38 students are male. What percent of the class is female?
    A. 42%
    B. 58%
    C. 56%
    D. 62%

12 — Four out of twenty-eight students in your class must go to summer school. What is the ratio of the classmates who do NOT go to summer school?
    A. 6/7
    B. 1/7
    C. 4/7
    D. 3/7

13 — What is the Greatest Common Factor (GCF) of 18 and 80?
    A. 2
    B. 3
    C. 9
    D. Cannot answer with the information provided

14 — What is the Least Common Multiple (LCM) of 7 and 13?
    A. 2
    B. 92
    C. 130
    D. Cannot answer with the information provided

15 — What is the value of 3!? (Note: the exclamation point in this question indicates factorial not excitement or surprise.)
    A. 0
    B. 2
    C. 6
    D. 127

16 — What is the Greatest Common Factor (GCF) of 5 and 75?
    A. 2
    B. 3
    C. 5
    D. 25

17 — What is the value of P? $P = (3^0 * 9^2) - (2^0 * 3^4)$
    A. -4
    B. 0
    C. 18
    D. Cannot determine from the information provided

18 — What is equivalent to 5^3?
    A. 5 * 3
    B. $5^1 * 5^1 * 5^1$
    C. $5^5 \div 2$
    D. None of the above

19 — If Jimmy got a grade of 85% on Homework A (that was worth 200 points), a 72% on Homework B (that was worth 150 points), a 45% on Homework C (that was worth 120 points), and a 98% on Homework D (that was worth 330 points), what was Jimmy's average grade? Round off your answer to the nearest percentage.
    A. 72%
    B. 78%
    C. 82%
    D. 86%

20 — A sweater went on sale and now costs $25.20. If the original price of the sweater was $42.00, what is the percent discount?

    A. 16.8%

    B. 20.0%

    C. 40.0%

    D. 60.0%

21 — Martha has a recipe for her mother's famous chocolate cake. Because Martha's family is quite a bit smaller than the family she grew up in, she decided to decrease the recipe by 20%. Later, she finds out that her husband had (without telling her) invited his boss and his boss's wife over for dinner at their house, and wants Martha to make a cake big enough for everyone. So Martha decides to increase the recipe back to its original amount. By what percentage does the recipe need to now be increased to bake her mother's chocolate cake?

    A. 12.5%

    B. 20%

    C. 25%

    D. 30%

22 — What would be the likely next number in the following pattern?   5, 5, 25, 6, 6, 36, ?

    A. 6

    B. 7

    C. 36

    D. Unable to answer from the information given

23 — Joe's house has appreciated in value by 7% every year for 4 years straight. If Joe paid $200,000 for his house, what is the value of Joe's house after 4 years (rounded off to the nearest dollar)?

    A. $214,000

    B. $245,045

    C. $262,159

    D. $281,100

24 — The combined ages of Jorge and his younger sister Alicia are 42. If their ages are separated by eight years, how old is Alicia?

    A. 25

    B. 32

    C. 17

    D. 11

25 — What mathematical property is exemplified in the following formula? $A * B = B * A$

    A. Distributive Property of Products

    B. Property of Products

    C. Commutative Property of Multiplication

    D. None of the above

26 — Moe went to the store and bought a bag of candy that contained 200 pieces. Moe will be distributing candy to his friends at his birthday party later that day. He will give exactly seven pieces of candy to each friend, and he has 23 friends that he has invited to his party. How many pieces of candy will Moe still have in his possession after giving away candy to his friends?

    A. 16

    B. 39

    C. 45

    D. 54

27 — Gourmet cookies are regularly priced at 89 cents if sold individually. How much is each cookie if one-and-a-half dozen sell for $12.89?

    A. 65 cents

    B. 82 cents

    C. 72 cents

    D. 80 cents

28 — What is the value of $x^{1/2} + x^{1/2}$ if $x = 9$?

    A. $\sqrt{18}$

    B. $2\sqrt{9}$

    C. 6

    D. Cannot determine from the information provided

29 — What is the equivalent of 7^5?
   A. 77,775
   B. $7^7 \div 7^2$
   C. $7^2 + 7^3$
   D. An irrational number

30 — What mathematical property is exemplified in the following formula? $A + B = B + A$
   A. Property of Addition Reversal
   B. Commutative Property of Addition
   C. Distributive Property of Addition
   D. None of the above

31 — Write the numerical equivalent of $3.57 * 10^8$.
   A. 35,700,000,000
   B. 35,700,000
   C. 3,570,000,000
   D. 357,000,000

32 — Write the decimal equivalent of $9.56 * 10^{-3}$.
   A. 0.00956
   B. 9560
   C. 956000
   D. 0.000956

33 — How much weight must you lose each week if you are determined to lose 63 pounds in 6 months?
   A. 0.4 lbs. per week
   B. 2.4 lbs. per week
   C. 1.4 lbs. per week
   D. 0.64 lbs. per week

34 — How much money must you save each week if you are determined to have $375 in the next 7 months?
   A. $12.38 per week
   B. $11.50 per week
   C. $13.75 per week
   D. $7. 75 per week

35 — If you think that you can save $450 out of your monthly paycheck, how long will it take for you to save $3995 for the down payment on a car? (Assume you receive your paycheck at the end of each month.)
   A. 8 months
   B. 10 months
   C. 9 weeks
   D. 9 months

36 — You have read that your car is losing value at a rate of $55 per month. You are asking $1790 and a potential buyer has offered you $1450. How many months will it take before it is to your benefit to accept that offer?
   A. 8 months
   B. 6 months
   C. 15 weeks
   D. 4 months

37 — What is the probability of selecting a black ace out of a complete deck of cards? (A complete deck contains 52 cards.)
   A. 1/2
   B. 1/13
   C. 1/26
   D. 1/4

38 — What is the probability of tossing a coin 6 times and getting a "head" each time?
   A. 1/32
   B. 1/16
   C. 1/8
   D. 1/64

9 — The probability of guessing correctly on a multiple-choice test or quiz answer is 1/4. What could you expect for a score if you guessed n all 10 questions on a multiple-choice quiz?

    A. 50%

    B. 70%

    C. 25%

    D. 10%

0 — If the probability of winning a weekly lottery is 1/1,600,000, what is your probability of winning once if you play the lottery every week for 5 years?

    A. $6.25 * 10^{-7}$

    B. 0.1625

    C. 0.0001625

    D. 1625/10000

Mathematics Knowledge

1 — If one solution to the quadratic equation $x^2 + 7x + 12 = 0$ is x = -3, what is the other possible value of x?
   A. -3
   B. -4
   C. 3
   D. 4

2 — Solve for k in the following equation: $64^k = 4^{15}$
   A. 2
   B. 3
   C. 5
   D. 15

3 — Find the two solutions to the following quadratic equation: $x^2 + 2x - 48 = 0$
   A. (-6, -8)
   B. (6, 8)
   C. (-6, 8)
   D. (6, -8)

4 — If 16x + 25 = -80, what is the value of x?
   A. 6.5625
   B. 6.6222
   C. 8.9520
   D. 1.2252

5 — An animal farm owner tried to count the number of animals he had. When he counted the heads, he counted a total of 200, but when he counted the total number of legs, he counted 540. If the farm has only chickens and cows, what is the total number of chickens?
   A. 120
   B. 130
   C. 140
   D. 150

6 — Tammy drives Car A, which is traveling at 50 miles/hour to the east on a perfectly straight road that goes exactly east-west. Tony drives Car B, which is traveling on the same road, at 30 miles/hour to the west. Tammy and Tony are 560 miles apart. How many miles will Tony drive before he passes Tammy?
   A. 180 miles
   B. 210 miles
   C. 240 miles
   D. 350 miles

7 — John is driving his car; he is traveling 65 miles/hour. Later, Julie tells John that she has built a toy rocket that is advertised as traveling 100 feet/second, and when she sets it off, it actually goes 95% of its advertised speed. Which goes faster, the car or the rocket, and by how much?
   A. Car; 5 feet/second difference
   B. Neither the car nor the toy rocket — they are traveling at about the same speed
   C. Rocket; 8 feet/second difference
   D. Rocket; 32 feet/second difference

8 — What is the median of the following data set? 1 2 5 5 5 6 7 90 78 45 61 32 56 90 98 108 1
   A. 5
   B. 29
   C. 32
   D. 51

9 — What is the mode of the following data set? 3 3.25 3.5 4 4.5 5 5 7 8 8 9.5 5.25 5
   A. 3
   B. 5
   C. 5.48

D. Unable to answer with the information provided

10 — What is the range in the following data set?   2 5 6 7 90 78 45 61 32 76 111 56 4 3
  A. 49.2
  B. 54.0
  C. 109
  D. 111

11 — Here are the monthly precipitation totals for Portland for the first half of 2015:

  January: 5.9 inches
  February: 6.1 inches
  March: 8.1 inches
  April: 2.0 inches
  May: 2.2 inches
  June: 0.9 inches

The monthly average precipitation for 2015 was 5 inches. What was the average precipitation during the second half of 2015?
  A. 4.2
  B. 5
  C. 5.8
  D. Unable to answer with the information provided

12 — The average of x and y is 8, and the average of y and z is 21. If x equals 6, what is the value of z?
  A. 8
  B. 18
  C. 22
  D. 32

13 — A six-sided die is rolled three times by Crazy John who has impulsively made a trip to Las Vegas.   What is the percentage probability that all three of the rolls are 5's or 6's?
  A. About 3.7%
  B. About 7.1%
  C. About 8.8%
  D. About 12.3%

14 — What is the area of a square that is 22.6 inches on a side? Give your answer in square feet.
  A. About 1.8 ft^2
  B. About 3.5 ft^2
  C. About 44 ft^2
  D. About 10 ft^2

15 — Circle 1 has a radius of 42 inches. Circle 2 has a radius that is 62% smaller than the radius of Circle 1. What is the area of Circle 2 as expressed in square feet?
  A. 14.8 ft^2
  B. 23.8 ft^2
  C. 126.2 ft^2
  D. 5,539 ft^2

16 — Judy must wrap five Christmas presents this year for her five sisters, so she goes out shopping for wrapping paper. She finds 22 square feet of beautiful wrapping paper at her local Target store. If the shape of all the presents will be a cube, and miraculously she uses almost all of the wrapping paper she buys, what is the maximum length possible of one side of the gift box?
  A. About 4.5 inches
  B. About 8.85 inches
  C. About 10.25 inches
  D. About 20 inches

17 — If y = 4, given the following equation, what is the value of x?   x = (2y - 5) ÷ 2
  A. 0.2
  B. 1.5
  C. 39

D. 40

18 — If two lines intersect, how many angles are formed?
   A. 1
   B. 2
   C. 4
   D. Between 1 and 4

19 — What is the angle measurement across a straight line?
   A. 90 degrees (90°)
   B. 180 degrees (180°)
   C. 360 degrees (360°)
   D. Cannot determine from the information provided

20 — What condition is necessary for a person to be able to calculate area?
   A. The figure exists in three dimensions
   B. The two-dimensional figure must be "closed"; i.e. a polygon, circle, etc.
   C. All four angles within the two-dimensional figures must add up to equal 180 degrees
   D. The figure must be defined by only two lines

21 — What are acute angles?
   A. Angles equal to 90°
   B. Angles less than 90 degrees (< 90°)
   C. Angles more than 90 degrees (> 90°)
   D. Angles formed by parallel lines

22 — How would you describe a triangle with Side A = 54 feet, Side B = 32 feet, and Side C = 54 feet?
   A. Equilateral triangle
   B. Anterior triangle
   C. Isosceles triangle
   D. Right triangle

23 — What is the sum of the three internal angles of any triangle?
   A. Can vary, but always < 90°
   B. Always 90°
   C. Can vary, but always > 90°
   D. Always 180°

24 — Given a right triangle with Side A = 20 ft and Side B = 15, and assuming that the meeting of Side A and Side B form the right angle, and assuming that Side C is the longest side, what is the length of Side C?
   A. Approximately 23 feet
   B. Approximately 38 feet
   C. $\sqrt{625}$ feet
   D. 625 feet

25 — What is the approximate radius of a circle, in yards, with a circumference of 190 feet?
   A. 6 yards
   B. 9 yards
   C. 10 yards
   D. 30 yards

26 — Circle A has a diameter of 100 miles; Circle B has a radius of 25 miles. How much larger is the area of Circle A than of Circle B?
   A. 2:1 or 200%
   B. 3.14:1 or about 314%
   C. 4:1 or 400%
   D. 12.56:1 or 1,256%

27 — Multiply the binomials (x+4) (2x-3).
   A. $2x^2 + 5x - 12$
   B. $x^2 + 5x - 12$
   C. $2x^2 - 5x + 12$

D. $x^2 - 4x - 12$

28 — Multiply the binomials $(x+4)(2x-2)$.

A. $2x^2 + 6x - 8$

B. $x^2 + 6x - 8$

C. $2x^2 - 6x + 8$

D. $x^2 - 4x - 8$

29 — A rectangle with a length and width of 3x and x, respectively, has an area of $3x^2$. Write the area polynomial when the length is increased by 5 units and the width is decreased by 3 units. So, to find the area, solve the following: $(3x+5)(x-3)$.

A. $3x^2 + 14x - 15$

B. $3x^2 - 4x - 15$

C. $3x^2 - 5x + 15$

D. $3x^2 + 4x - 15$

30 — A triangle with a base and height of 4x and 7x, respectively has an area of $14x^2$, which is equal to 1/2 times the base times the height. Write the area polynomial when the base is increased by 2 units and the height is increased by 3 units. So, to find the area, solve the following: $1/2(4x+2)(7x+3)$.

A. $14x^2 + 14x + 6$

B. $14x^2 + 14x + 3$

C. $14x^2 + 13x + 3$

D. $14x^2 + 28x + 3$

31 — What value of x will satisfy the inequality $14x - 8 > 24$?

A. $x > 7/16$

B. $x > 16/7$

C. $x < 16/7$

D. $x < 7/16$

32 — What value of x will satisfy the inequality $5x + 16 < 49$?

A. $x > 33/5$

B. $x > 5/33$

C. $x < 33/5$

D. $x < 5/33$

Vocabulary

1 — D. Soften

Macerate means to cause to become soft or separated into constituent elements by or as if by steeping in liquid; steep; soak; to soften or wear away, especially as a result of being wetted.

2 — C. Bag

Pouch means a small drawstring bag carried on the person for transporting goods.

3 — B. Belief

Tenet means a principle, belief, or doctrine held to be true.

4 — D. Across

Transverse means acting, lying, or being across; set crosswise; made at right angles to the anterior-posterior axis of the body.

5 — C. Giving

Bounteous means giving or disposed to give freely; liberally bestowed.

6 — D. Case

Sheath means a case for a blade (as of a knife).

7 — C. Gadget

Doodad means a small article whose common name is unknown or forgotten; gadget; an ornamental attachment or decoration.

8 — D. Grand

Grandiose means characterized by affectation of grandeur of splendor or by absurd exaggeration.

9 — A. Hodgepodge

Pastiche means a literary, artistic, or musical work that imitates the style of previous work or that has a composition made up of selections from different works; potpourri; hodgepodge.

10 — A. Copy

Replica means a close reproduction or facsimile, especially by a maker of the original; copy; duplicate; reproduction.

11 — C. Zany

Screwball means crazily eccentric or whimsical; zany.

12 — C. Pronouncement

Dictum means a formal, authoritative pronouncement of a principle, proposition, or opinion.

13 — B. Devise

Formulate means to put into a systematized statement or expression; devise; to prepare something according to formula.

14 — B. Jovial

Jolly means full of high spirits; joyous; given to conviviality; jovial; expressing, suggesting, or inspiring gaiety; cheerful; splendid.

15 — D. Digestive

Peptic means relating to or promoting digestion.

16 — B. Intemperate

Shrill means having a vivid or sharp effect on the senses; strident; intemperate; having or emitting a sharp, high-pitched tone or sound; piercing.

17 — B. Plot

Collude means to conspire; plot.

18 — D. Plead

Entreat means to plead with especially to persuade; ask urgently; negotiate; intercede.

19 — C. Sensational
Melodramatic means appealing to the emotions; sensational.

20 — C. Primitive
Primal means original; primitive; first in importance; fundamental.

21 — B. Negligent
Slack means not using due diligence, care, or dispatch; negligent; characterized by slowness, sluggishness, or lack of energy; moderate in some quality.

22 — D. Contravene
Thwart means to run counter so as to effectively baffle or oppose; contravene; defeats the hopes and aspirations of.

23 — B. Malice
Grudge means a feeling of deep-seated resentment or ill will; malice.

24 — C. Dynamic
Kinetic means of or relating to the motion of material bodies and the associated forces and energy; active; lively; dynamic; energizing.

25 — D. Repeat
Parrot means to repeat by rote.

26 — C. Brook
Rivulet means a small stream; brook.

27 — B. Immerse
Souse means to plunge in liquid; immerse; drench; saturate.

28 — D. Support
Buttress means a projecting support built into a wall; something that supports or strengthens.

29 — B. Unfeeling
Callous means unfeeling; emotionally hardened; insensitive; indifferent; unsympathetic.

30 — A. Impulsive
Impetuous means impulsive; rushing with force and violence; hasty; of, relating to, or characterized by sudden or rash action or emotion.

31 — C. Intensely
Vehemently means intensely; forcefully; powerfully; zealously; ardently; with passion; angrily; emotionally.

32 — B. Explain
Elucidate means to explain; to clarify; to throw light upon; to illuminate; to clear up.

33 — A. Deceit
Guile means deceit; duplicity; double-dealing; insidious cunning in attaining a goal; crafty or artful deception.

34 — C. Roomy
Commodious means roomy; spacious; convenient; ample or adequate for a particular purpose.

35 — A. Cause
Engender means to cause; to produce; to give rise to; to beget; to procreate; to come into existence.

Critical Reading

1 — C. The working poor
The working poor are the main subject of this paragraph, which the speaker develops at length in her argument of what it means to be a member of this group.

2 — D. All of the above
The speaker provides an extensive definition of exactly what it means to be the "working poor" by comparing and contrasting their deprivation with the comfortable lives of the privileged people they serve. In so doing, she is establishing an emotional appeal for their plight.

3 — B. Blunt and sympathetic
The speaker is very sympathetic to the plight of the working poor and she is very straightforward in her language when discussing the details of their deprived lives. She speaks in very concrete terms of the ways in which they suffer to ensure that the more privileged members of society can live a comfortable existence.

4 — C. Because it is a formal term to describe a common group found in society today
The speaker puts the term in quotation marks to make her audience understand that she has not coined it; rather, it is a term given (probably by economists) to describe the group of people who fit the definition that she expounds upon in the paragraph.

5 — D. They make the lives of the wealthy simpler and more enjoyable
The main thrust of this paragraph is the notion that the working poor give so much of themselves so that more privileged members of society can live a good life. They probably do make society function more smoothly, but that is not expressly stated in the paragraph. They are certainly not lazy, and though the speaker mentions that these working parents probably do neglect their own children, it is merely because they are too busy taking care of other people's children, not because they are inherently neglectful parents.

6 — C. Illness is possible to avoid
While all those statements are made in one way or another by the speaker, the main point is that illness is avoidable, despite how impossible that notion may seem.

7 — D. Both A and B
By using the second person pronoun, you, the speaker achieves an informal conversational style, while also directly addressing his audience, thereby making them feel personally involved in the discussion. Though the speaker seemingly is going to impart knowledge to his audience in subsequent paragraphs, in no way is his tone lecturing, but rather engaging and encouraging of contemplation.

8 — C. Hypotheticals
The speaker neither outlines a process nor uses cause and effect to build his argument, but rather relies heavily on the use of hypothetical examples to help his audience visualize the potentiality of ending illness completely, and dying a natural death at a very old age.

9 — B. "End of illness"
The speaker wishes "it" for his reader, meaning the "end of illness".

10 — A. Contemplative
The speaker considers several hypothetical scenarios of the way a person may die without suffering and at a very old age, and from those, he poses the notion that we may all experience end of life in such a way. Therefore, more than the other choices, the speaker is contemplative of the possibilities of the end of illness. He addresses his audience directly in an engaging manner, not in a serious didactic tone. He is certain the end of illness is possible; therefore, he does not doubt it. When speaking of death, he speaks plainly, positively declaring that without illness, it is nothing to fear. Therefore, he is not morose.

11 — C. Assimilation helps us determine which groups are less worthy than others
The speaker tells us the exact opposite about the worthiness of certain groups. In fact, he argues that all groups are equally worthy and should not be forced into assimilation merely because they are different than the rest. The other statements are all true, according to the speaker.

12 — A. Critical
The speaker is critical of the way that assimilation is often forced on certain groups, for no legitimate reason. But he does not mock, or satirize, this practice, nor does he downplay his own accomplishments or achievements (self-effacing).

3 — D. Assimilation forces us to be both self-aware and aware of others simultaneously

The paradox to which the speaker specifically refers is that the act of conforming to certain societal norms forces us to consider the needs of others, yet it also helps us develop our own selves; thus, achieving "a broader mindfulness," which also helps us "to elaborate ourselves as individuals."

4 — A. Formal

The speaker's style can most accurately be described as formal; his tone is appropriately serious due to the serious nature of this topic and his language is reflective of the gravity of the subject matter, as well as its academic nature. Yet, he is not overly formal enough to be characterized as grandiloquent; the speaker writes in a way that is accessible to a wide audience. Nor is his style colloquial, in that he does not use regional dialects or language that tends to slanginess or excessive informality. Lastly, his style cannot be described as lyrical; it is not sing-songy or poetic in sound.

5 — A. Requiring that all men keep their hair cut short

Only choice A, requiring men keep their hair cut short, would be an example of coerced assimilation, or blending in with a societal norm or expectation of what, in this case, a man should look like. Segregation is, in a way, the opposite of assimilation, as one group would purposely NOT be allowed to assimilate into another group of society. Women having their heads covered is not so much forced assimilation, but rather mandated behavior that certain societal leaders have determined is appropriate for women, which is not based on assimilation, but rather, again, separation from other members or groups due to gender.

Arithmetic Reasoning

1 — A. =

Any integer with zero as its exponent has a value of one (1). The question is asking, "Is one equal to, greater than, or less than one?", or "none of the above." It is important to remember this example because no matter how large or complex the base, the zero exponent means the value is 1.

2 — B. 5.625

If Q = 4.5, and Y is half of Q (or Y is 50% of Q), then:

Y = Q * 0.5 = 4.5 * 0.5 = 2.25

And if X is 250% of Y (or X is 2.5 times the value of Y), then:

X = 2.25 * 2.5 = 5.625

3 — C. 4,305

Note that the correct answer must be larger than 861, because it states that 861 is 20% of some number. You could get the correct answer in two ways.

First, consider that if the number given is 20% of a larger number, you need to multiply the given number by 5 (0.2 is 5 times less than 100%). Therefore, 500% of the given number is 861 * 5 or 4,305.

Second, you may consider solving the following equation (0.2 is the decimal value of 20%):

$861 = f * 0.2$
$861/0.2 = (f * 0.2)/0.2$
$4,305 = f$

4 — D. 75%

You may want to first interpret this question in mathematics terms. "What percentage" means that you will find a value that will be divided by 100. "Of" indicates multiplication will be used. "Is 15" can be translated as "equals 15".

So, applying these terms together in logical order, the question can be expressed as the following equation:

$(f/100) * 20 = 15$
$[(f/100) * 20] \div 20 = 15 \div 20$
$f/100 = 0.75$
$f = 75$

You could also find the answer as a decimal, and then translate it into a percentage.

$f = 15/20$
$f = 0.75$
$f = 75\%$

5 — C. Distributive Property

This very important mathematical property is easy to remember if you keep in mind that "multiplication distributes over addition" — take the number inside the parentheses or factor the number out. If you were to place numbers within the formula, the following would be an example of multiplication distributing over addition:

$10(3 + 6) = (10 * 3) + (10 * 6)$
$10 * 9 = 30 + 60$
$90 = 90$

Here is an example of "factoring" based on the Distributive Property:

4x - 8 = 4(x - 2)

The idea of factoring a value out of an expression is based on the ability to see common factors.
In this example 4 is a factor of both 4 and the 8, so it can be taken outside of parentheses.

6 — C. 37

The sequence of numbers is determined by the following formula, beginning with 1 and continuing with each whole number:

$x^2 + 1$

Now, if you substitute those values into the formula, you would find the following (desired) numbers:

$1^2 + 1 = 2$
$2^2 + 1 = 5$
$3^2 + 1 = 10$
$4^2 + 1 = 17$
$5^2 + 1 = 26$
$6^2 + 1 = 37$

There is no one specific way to solve pattern problems. You may be able to search for the patterns in the most logical and sequential method that you find useful. For example, the given pattern :

2, 5, 10, 17, 26, ?

may be solved in the following way:

Looking at this sequence of numbers and adding numbers, another pattern appears,

2 + 3 = 5
5 + 5 = 10
10 + 7 = 17
17 + 9 = 26

Using this approach, we can see that we have used increasing odd numbers to add to the sequence numbers to predict the following sequence value. For that reason our next value must be:

26 + 11 = 37

This matches our previous example but here we were able to solve without predicting a formula. The answer does not require a formula, it just needs the next number in sequence. The second method allows us to use "mental math" to predict the next number. The result is a correct answer either way.

7 — A. Associative Property of Multiplication

The Associative Property of Multiplication is a basic property that is important to understand and be able to apply. The word "associative" means "to group". If you were to place numbers within the formula, the following would be an example:

18 * (3 * 6) = (18 * 3) * 6
18 * 18 = 54 * 6
324 = 324

It simply says that multiplication can be grouped in various ways without changing the outcome.

8 — C. 4.7

The absolute value of a number is its distance relative to 0 on a number line; therefore, all absolute values are positive numbers. The following is a more formal definition: "a term used in mathematics to indicate the distance of a point or number from the origin (zero) of a number line or coordinate system; this can apply to scalar or vector quantities."

If written numerically, the absolute value of a number is indicated by thin vertical lines on either side of the number. The absolute value of 8 is 8, and the absolute value of -8 also equals 8. The absolute value will always be a positive value.

9 — D. All of the above

In mathematics, the reciprocal of a number x is 1/x. The reciprocal of x when multiplied by x gives a product of 1. It is sometimes called the "multiplicative inverse." For example, the reciprocal of five is one-fifth (or 0.2); the reciprocal of 1/4 (0.25) is four. Note that zero does not have a reciprocal because no real number multiplied by 0 equals 1.

This is a concept that will appear in some way, so be able to recall the property of the reciprocal.

10 — D. 88.8%

5 * 0.91 = 4.55. Adding your latest test: 4.55 + 0.78 = 5.33; your new percentage is 5.33/6 = 0.888, or 88.8%.

11 — B. 58%

Since 16 of the students are male, 38 – 16, or 22, of the students are female. 22/38 = 0.5789 which is the fraction of females. 0.58 is 58% which is the percent.

12 — A. 6/7

The ratio of students who will NOT go is 24/28 or 6/7.

13 — A. 2

The Greatest Common Factor (GCF) is found by identifying all of the factors of the two or more numbers in your set, and then finding the largest number that they share.

Factors of 18 =1, 2, 3, 6, 9, 18
Factors of 80 =1, 2, 4, 5, 8, 10, 16, 20, 40, 80

The greatest (largest) common factor shared by these two numbers is 2.

14 — C. 130

The Least Common Multiple (LCM) is found by finding all of the numbers that are multiples of the given number. Simply multiply the given number by all of the integers (1, 2, 3, 4, 5, 6 etc.):

For 7 — 7, 14, 21, 28, 35, 42, 49, 56, 63, 70, 81, 88, 95, 102, 109, 116, 123, 130, 137, etc.
For 13 — 13, 26, 39, 52, 65, 78, 91, 104, 117, 130, 143, 156, etc.

The LCM for 7 and 13 would be 130 which is the smallest number that appears in both lists.

15 — C. 6

The use of the exclamation sign attached to a number is mathematical, and it may be on the test, so make sure you are familiar on how to use it and earn some easy points on the exam. The exclamation point following a number indicates the "factorial" operation. It simply means multiply all of the integers up to and including that number.

3! = 1 * 2 * 3 = 6

16 — C. 5

The Greatest Common Factor (GCF) is found by identifying all of the factors of the two or more numbers in your set, and then finding the largest number that they share.

Factors of 5 = 1, 5
Factors of 75 = 1, 3, 5, 15, 25, 75

the greatest (largest) common factor these two numbers share is 5.

7 — B. 0
The key here is to recall that any number with zero as its exponent equals one.

$9^0 = 1$
$2^0 = 1$

Substituting these values into the equation:

$? = (3^0 * 9^2) - (2^0 * 3^4)$
$? = (1 * 9^2) - (1 * 3^4)$
$? = 9^2 - 3^4$
$? = (9 * 9) - (3 * 3 * 3 * 3)$
$? = 81 - 81$
$? = 0$

18 — B. $5^1 * 5^1 * 5^1$
Recall that any number to the 1st power (for example, x1) simply equals itself.
$5^3 = 5 * 5 * 5$
$5^3 = 5^1 * 5^1 * 5^1$

19 — C. 82%
First, you want to find how many points Jimmy earned on his four homework assignments:'

Homework 1: 200 * 0.85 = 170 points
Homework 2: 150 * 0.72 = 108 points
Homework 3: 120 * 0.45 = 54 points
Homework 4: 330 * 0.98 = 323 points

If you add those points together, you get the total number of points that Jimmy earned:

170 + 108 + 54 + 323 = 655 total points

Next, you want to find out how many points were possible by adding the points for each of the four homework assignments:

200 + 150 + 120 + 330 = 800 total possible points

Therefore, to calculate the average, you divide the points earned by the points possible:

655 ÷ 800 = 0.819 = about 0.82 = 82%

After doing very badly on Homework 3 (thankfully, it wasn't worth many points), Jimmy did very well on Homework 4 to bring his average for his homework assignments up to 82%.

20 — C. 40.0%
Any "before-to-after" question can be expressed as either a ratio or as a fraction. In this case, the ratio would be 25.2:42; i.e. the "new price" compared to the "original price". The equivalent fraction would be expressed by dividing: 25.2 ÷ 42. If you divide these numbers, you get 0.6. Any decimal can be converted to a percentage by multiplying by 100, so 0.6 means you paid 60% of the original price of the sweater. However, the question is asking for the "percent discount", and this means something different; the difference between the original price and the discounted price. (The answer requires the percent discount, which is the amount less than 100% of the original price.) To get this, subtract 60% from 100%. Here, the sale price is 40% less than the original price, so the "percent discount" is 40%.

21 — C. 25%
Martha's "newer" recipe was 20% (or 0.2) less than her "older" recipe. According to the question, Martha's "newer" recipe will then be increased such that she will now be making the same amount of cake as what was described in her original

recipe. But note that the question is asking "by what percentage" does the "newer" recipe need to be increased to make the recipe that wil[l] accommodate her guests.

Martha's "older"/original recipe was 100%; so perhaps it used 100 tablespoons of milk. Her "newer" recipe would use 20% less, so it uses 8[0] tablespoons of milk, or 80% of the original 100 tablespoons of milk (100 * 0.8 = 80).

In the second step, however, the question requires Martha to add an amount of milk that brings the quantity up to the same as the origina[l] amount in her recipe. Martha needs to return to the original quantity of 100 tablespoons of milk. She can write the following down, usin[g] the symbol ß for the number of tablespoons of milk she now needs to add:

$80 + ß = 100$
$ß = 20$

The question is the following: "By what percentage will 80 be increased if she adds 20?" Since 20 is 25% of 80, 25% of 80 tablespoons nee[d] to be added to get back to the original one hundred. Therefore, the correct answer is 25%.

---

22 — B. 7

The sequence of numbers is determined by observing that there is a pair of identical numbers, followed by multiplying them together, fol-lowed by the next whole number following the initial number in the series, followed by multiplying them together. The most likely nex[t] number would follow the same pattern; the next number after 6 is 7.

---

23 — C. $262,159

"Appreciates" means that the value of the house increases each year by a fixed percentage. If you are using percentages, and those percentage[s] are expressed as decimals, you will need to multiply. For example, if something goes up by 20%, you can multiply that given number by 20% and add that number to the original value. It is simpler to multiply the original number by 1.2. You may find this process faster since it i[s] one operation and not two.

Here is Joe's situation:

Beginning of Year 0 (the starting point) = 200,000.00
Beginning of Year 1 (200,000 * 1.07) = 214,000.00
Beginning of Year 2 (214,000 * 1.07) = 228,980.00
Beginning of Year 3 (228,980 * 1.07) = 245,008.60
Beginning of Year 4 (245,008.6 * 1.07) = 262,159.20

Joe's house, 4 years after he bought it, is now valued at $262,159.20, an increase of $62,159.20!

To solve this problem, the percentage increase must be applied to the new value each year, not just to the original price. It assumes that th[e] percentage increase is applied in yearly increments. If the percent increase is applied every month by 0.833% each month (found by 7%/12 or 0.07/12 = 0.833) the total value at the end of 4 years would be slightly different (it would be even more).

If you simply applied a 7% increase to the original price for 4 years, Joe would "earn" a lesser amount, as show here:

Beginning of Year 0 (the starting point) = 200,000.00
Beginning of Year 1 (200,000 * 1.07) = 214,000.00 ($14,000 added each year)
Beginning of Year 2 (214,000 + 14,000) = 228,000
Beginning of Year 3 (228,000 + 14,000) = 242,000
Beginning of Year 4 (242,000 + 14,000) = 256,000

Under this "plan", Joe would have "lost" $6,159.2. This is a great example of one of the most important concepts: the power of compound interest.

---

24 — C. 17

21 + 21 = 42 (if they were the same age); if you separate them by 4 each way (4 + 4 = 8), then 21+ 4 = 25 and 21 − 4 = 17; Checking you[r] work, 17 is indeed 8 years less than 25, matching the problem's stipulation that Alicia is 8 years younger than Jorge.

25 — C. Commutative Property of Multiplication

The Commutative Property of Multiplication is one of three basic properties of multiplying numbers and is very important to understand and apply. The word "commute" means "to move around", and so this property refers to moving numbers around within an equation. An example of this property is the following:

$6 * 7 = 7 * 6$

Commutative Property means that the order of operation can be reversed without affecting the outcome.

26 — B. 39

Moe has 23 friends and gives them 7 pieces of candy each; therefore, he gives away 161 pieces total. 200 - 161 = 39 pieces left over.

27 — C. 72 cents

12.89/18 = .7161, and this is "rounded up" to the nearest cent.

28 — C. 6

A fractional exponent is equivalent to the root of the number. The exponent 1/2, is equivalent to the square root. Therefore, $x^{1/2} = \sqrt{x}$.

$9^{1/2} = \sqrt{9}$

$\sqrt{9} + \sqrt{9}$

$3 + 3$

6

29 — B. $7^7 \div 7^2$

The value of 7^5 is not hard to calculate:

$7^5 = 7 * 7 * 7 * 7 * 7 = 16,807$

This makes it easy to immediately eliminate answer choice A. Now, find the value of answer choice B:

$7^7 \div 7^2 = (7 * 7 * 7 * 7 * 7 * 7 * 7) \div (7 * 7) = 823,543 \div 49 = 16,807$

There's the correct answer. Just to make sure, you may want to look at answer choice C.:

$7^2 + 7^3 = (7 * 7) + (7 * 7 * 7) = 49 + 343 = 392$

Of course, the answer can't be an irrational number since it involves exponential values.

30 — B. Commutative Property of Addition

The Commutative Property of Addition of one of three basic properties of adding numbers and so it is very important to understand and be able to apply it. The word "commute" means "to move around", and so this property refers to moving numbers around within an equation. An example of this property is the following:

$2 + 4 = 4 + 2$

The Commutative Property of Addition says that the order of operation for addition can be changed without changing the result of the operation.

31 — D. 357,000,000

The number $3.57 * 10^8$ in scientific notation will convert to the number 357 followed by a number of zeros. That number of zeros is determined by counting from the decimal in 3.57, eight places to the right. That means the correct value is 357,000,000, or answer D.

32 — A. 0.00956

The number $9.56 * 10^{-3}$ in scientific notation will convert to the number 956 with the decimal place moved three places to the left. That means the correct value is 0.00956, or answer A.

33 — B. 2.4 lbs. per week

Six months is half of a year and a year is 52 weeks. The rate will be determined by dividing the total amount by 26 weeks. The rate is therefore 63/26, or about 2.4 pounds per week.

34 — A. $12.38 per week

Seven months out of a year is 52 * 7/12 weeks = 30.3 weeks. The rate will therefore be determined by dividing the total amount ($375) by 30.3 weeks. The amount you must save per week is therefore $375/30.3 weeks, or about $12.38 per week.

35 — D. 9 months

3995 dollars divided by 450 dollars per month will provide an answer in months. Numerically, the value of that ratio is about 8.88. Since that partial month can't be used (because you are paid your entire paycheck once a month at the end of the month), it means that a full nine months will be required to get the full amount.

36 — B. 6 months

The difference between the offer and your asking price is $1790 – $1450, or $340. Dividing that value by the monthly decrease equals 340/55, or about 6.18 months. Rounding that value to 6 months, you can now evaluate the acceptability of the reduced offer. Since the partial month can be used as part of your decision process, rounding down to the six months is somewhat a judgment for the seller on the value of the money compared to the value of the car.

37 — C. 1/26

The ratio of correct choices to the total number of choices is how we determine the probability. In this case, that ratio is 2 black aces / 52 cards, or 1/26.

38 — D. 1/64

The ratio of correct choices to the total number of choices for each coin toss is 1/2. For a repetitive set of trials, the overall probability is 1/2 times 1/2 for the number of trials. For this example, with six trials, our total probability is 1/2 * 1/2 * 1/2 * 1/2 * 1/2 * 1/2, or 1/64.

39 — C. 25%

The probability of being correct for each question is 1/4 or 25%. Assuming that there is NO partial credit, 25% of the 10 questions means you could expect to be correct on 2.5 questions. That means that your expected score would be around 25% for the whole quiz.

40 — C. 0.0001625

Each of those weekly probabilities for winning is an independent event. In 5 years, you will play 5 times 52 weekly events. That means your probability of winning will be 260 times 1/1,600,000. That probability is 0.0001625, which is still extremely small. It is a probability of just over 1 in ten thousand.

Mathematics Knowledge

— B. -4

The given quadratic equation: $x^2 + 7x + 12 = 0$

Can be written as a quadratic equation in the form of $x^2 + x(a + b) + ab = 0$

Where a and b are the two roots of the equation. It can also be expressed as the product of those two terms: $(x + a)(x + b) = 0$

Therefore the equation, $x^2 + 7x + 12 = 0$ becomes: $(x + 3)(x + 4) = 0$

The product of these two factors equals zero only when one or the other factor is equal to 0.

If $x + 3 = 0$, then $x = -3$ (the one given possible value of x in the problem statement).
If $x + 4 = 0$, then $x = -4$ (the other value of x).

2 — C. 5

The first step is to convert both sides of the equation so that they both have the same base; therefore, you need to convert 64k to the base of 4 to some power.

If: $64 = 4 * 4 * 4 = 4^3$

Then: $64^k = (43)k$ or 4^{3k}

Now the original equation becomes: $4^{3k} = 4^{15}$

Since the bases are now the same, the equality means the two exponents of those bases must be equal. So you can conclude that if $3k = 15$, then $k = 5$.

3 — D. (6, -8)

This is a quadratic equation. It can be expressed as $x^2 + (a - b)x - ab = 0$

$x^2 + 2x - 48 = 0$
$x^2 + 8x - 6x - 48 = 0$
$x(x + 8) - 6(x + 8) = 0$
$(x + 8)(x - 6) = 0$

The product of these two factors equals zero only when the value of x is 6 or -8.

4 — A. 6.5625

$16x + 25 = -80$
$16x = -105$
$x = 6.5625$

5 — B. 130

If the number of chickens equals x, then the number of cows equals 200 - x. Remember that cows have 4 legs and chickens have 2 legs.

$2x + 4(200 - x) = 540$
$2x + 800 - 4x = 540$
$-2x = -260$
$2x = 260$
$x = 130$

6 — B. 210 miles

In one hour, Tammy drives 50 miles east and Tony drives 30 miles west. Together they have traveled a total of 80 miles. To travel 560 miles, they would need to drive for 7 hours (560 ÷ 80). After 7 hours, Tony would have driven 210 miles (30 * 7).

It may be good for you to check your answer. After the same 7 hours, Tammy would have driven 350 miles (50 * 7). If, after 7 hours, Tammy will have driven 350 miles and Tony will have driven 210 miles, together they would have "covered" the entire 560 (350 + 210) miles that they were originally separated.

7 — B. Neither the car nor the toy rocket — they are traveling at about the same speed

The most important thing in this problem is to convert the units for the car and the rocket so that they are exactly the same — the following factors allow the comparison:

5,280 feet are in a mile
60 minutes are in an hour.
60 seconds are in a minute.

The speed of the car is 65 miles/hour or:

65 * 5,280 = 343,200 feet/hour
343,200 ÷ 60 = 5,720 feet/minute
5,720 ÷ 60 = 95.3 feet/second, or about 95 feet/second

The advertised speed of the toy rocket is 100 feet/second. The actual speed is 95% of that, so:

100 feet/second * 0.95 = 95 feet/second

Therefore, the car and the toy rocket are traveling at approximately the same speed.

8 — C. 32

The median value of the set is the one that appears in the middle when the set is ordered from least to greatest. The median is NOT the average. Therefore, the first step in finding the mean is to put the numbers in the correct order:

1 1 2 5 5 5 6 7 32 45 56 61 78 90 90 98 108

There is an odd number of numbers (17) in the data set; this means that the median will be the "central" number. If you wanted to be really methodical, you could "chop" one number from each end until you get to the "center":

$$1\ 1\ 2\ 5\ 5\ 5\ 6\ 7\ 32\ 45\ 56\ 61\ 78\ 90\ 90\ 98\ 108$$
$$1\ 2\ 5\ 5\ 5\ 6\ 7\ 32\ 45\ 56\ 61\ 78\ 90\ 90\ 98$$
$$2\ 5\ 5\ 5\ 6\ 7\ 32\ 45\ 56\ 61\ 78\ 90\ 90$$
$$5\ 5\ 5\ 6\ 7\ 32\ 45\ 56\ 61\ 78\ 90$$
$$5\ 5\ 6\ 7\ 32\ 45\ 56\ 61\ 78$$
$$5\ 6\ 7\ 32\ 45\ 56\ 61$$
$$6\ 7\ 32\ 45\ 56$$
$$7\ 32\ 45$$
$$32$$

It is, of course, much easier to simply count the number of numbers, and then divide that sum by the number of numbers. In this case, there are 17 numbers, and so the "central" number will be the 9th one. The 9th number is 32!

9 — B. 5

The mode of a data set is simply the number that appears the most often in a data set. The most frequent number in this data set, 5, appears three times.

10 — C. 109

The range of a data set is the distance between the highest and the lowest values within the set. You simply need to find the smallest number and the largest number and find the difference by subtracting. In this data set, 2 is the smallest number and 111 is the largest number. Therefore, the range is 109 (111 - 2).

11 — C. 5.8

First, add up the precipitation for the six months that you do know:

5.9 + 6.1 + 8.1 + 2.0 + 2.2 + 0.9 = 25.2 inches

If the average for the entire year was 5 inches/month, and there are 12 months/year, the total amount of precipitation for the year can be calculated:

$T_{inches/year}$ = 5 inches/month * 12 months = 60 inches

$T_{July-December}$ = 60.0 - 25.2 = 34.8 inches

The average monthly precipitation for the second half of 2015 can now be calculated:

Average precipitation for July through December

= 34.8 inches ÷ 6 months
= 5.8 average inches/month

12 — D. 32
An average of two numbers can be found by adding them, and then dividing the sum by 2. Therefore, you can set up the following formulas:

8 = (x + y)/2
21 = (y + z)/2

Now you insert the value of x that you are given, which is 6, into the first formula:

8 = (x + y)/2
8 = (6 + y)/2
8 * 2 = [(6 + y)/2] * 2
16 = 6 + y
10 = y

Now that you have found the value for y, you can insert that into the second formula to get the value of z:

21 = (y + z)/2
21 * 2 = [(10 + z)/2] * 2
42 = 10 + z
32 = z

13 — A. About 3.7%
There is a 2:6 or 1:3 or 1/3rd chance that Crazy John will roll a 5 or a 6 every time he rolls the dice. One-third, expressed as a decimal, is equal to about 0.333. So, on the first role he has a 33.3% chance to roll one of his two favorite numbers. On the second roll, he again has a 33.3% chance of rolling 5's or 6's, so a 1/3rd chance of the 1/3rd chance. This would equal 0.333 * 0.333 = about 0.111 or about an 11.1% chance. For the third roll, the pattern would continue. On the third roll, he would have a 1/3 chance of 1/3 chance of 1/3 chance; therefore, 0.333 * 0.333 * 0.333 = about 0.0369, or 3.69% chance, and that is rounded to 3.7% chance.

14 — B. About 3.5 ft²
Notice that the information is given in inches and the answer needs to be given in feet.

A = L * W or L * L = L²

Since the length of a square and the width of a square are equal:

A_{square} = 22.6 * 22.6 = 22.62 = 510.76 inches²

This answer now needs to be converted to feet².

1 ft² = 12 inches * 12 inches or 144 inches²

You can now use this to convert your answer to the required units.

$A_{square} = (510.76$ inches$^2) \div 1$ feet$^2/144$ inches$^2 = 3.55$ ft^2
$A_{square} =$ about 3.5 ft^2

15 — A. 14.8 ft²
The area of a circle is determined using the following formula:

$A = (\pi)r^2$ so
$A_{circle\ 1} = (\pi)(42$ inches$)^2$
$A_{circle\ 1} = (3.14)(42 * 42)$
$A_{circle\ 1} = 3.14 * 1,764$
$A_{circle\ 1} = 5,539$ inches^2

Circle 2 does NOT have an area that is 62% less than Circle 1 — it has a radius that is 62% of Circle 1.

$R_{circle\ 2} = 42 * 0.62 = 26.04$ inches^2
$A_{circle\ 2} = (\pi)(26.04$ inches$)^2$
$A_{circle\ 2} = (3.14)(26.04 * 26.04)$
$A_{circle\ 2} = 3.14 * 678.08$
$A_{circle\ 2} = 2,129$ inches^2

The question asks you to give your answer in square feet. The conversion is 1 ft^2 = 12 inches * 12 inches = 144 inches^2.

$A_{circle\ 2} = 2,129$ inches$^2 * 1$ ft$^2/144$ inches^2
$A_{circle\ 2} = 2,129$ inches$^2 \div 144$ inches^2
$A_{circle\ 2} = 14.79$ ft^2, or about 14.8 ft^2

16 — C. About 10.25 inches
Judy bought 22 square feet of wrapping paper. She realizes that this equals 3,168 inches^2 of wrapping paper (22 ft^2 * 144 inches$^2/1$ ft^2) — she loves doing math!

There are 5 presents, and the presents are cubes. Each cube has 6 sides/faces, and so Judy must wrap 30 sides. If L = the length of one side of a cube, the area of each side/face of a cube is equal to L^2. Remember that L is the unknown that you are solving for.

Judy has 633.6 inches^2 for each cube (3,168 inches^2 * 1/5). Therefore, she has 105 inches^2 for each of the cube's sides/faces (633.6 inches$^2 \div 6$).

Since $A = L^2$ for a square:

105 inches$^2 = L^2 \sqrt{105} = L10.25$ inches = L

17 — B. 1.5
Substitute the known value of y into the given equation:

$x = (2y - 5) \div 2x = [(2 * 4) - 5] \div 2$
$x = (8 - 5) \div 2$
$x = 3 \div 2$
$x = 1.5$

18 — C. 4
Two lines intersect at a single point, The measurement between the rays formed from the point of intersection is called an angle. The unit of measurement for angles is degrees, which is indicated with the symbol ° following a number. Degree measurements show the magnitude of the "sweep" of the angle.

19 — B. 180 degrees (180°)
If you imagine a line "sweeping", in a circular motion, from one point on a line to another point on the same line, you could envision it as describing half of a circle. The angle of a rotating line that ends where it began is 360°, and half of that

...ould be 180º.

0 — B. The two-dimensional figure must be "closed"; i.e. a polygon, circle, etc.

If the geometrical figure is not "closed", i.e. it is not a polygon, circle, oval, etc., it will not be possible to measure the area enclosed by the figure.

1 — B. Angles less than 90 degrees (< 90º)

The definition of an acute angle is any angle greater than 0º and less than 90º.

2 — C. Isosceles triangle

If two of the three sides of any triangle are equal in length, it is described as an isosceles triangle.

3 — D. Always 180º

No matter what the shape of any triangle is, the sum of the three interior angles will always equal 180º. For example, an equilateral triangle has three interior angles of 60º each, and 60º * 3 = 180º. And even if you have a triangle with three different side lengths, the sum of its three interior angles will always be 180º.

4 — C. √625 feet

To answer this question, you need to know a very important geometry formula that is called the Pythagorean Theorem. The formula applies only to right triangles; i.e. a triangle where two of the sides form a right angle. The formula is expressed in this way:

$$C^2 = A^2 + B^2$$
$$C^2 = 20^2 + 15^2$$
$$C^2 = 400 + 225$$
$$C^2 = 625$$
$$C = \sqrt{625}$$

Side A and Side B form the right angle and Side C is the hypotenuse of the triangle. A component of the Pythagorean Theorem is that the sum of the areas of the two squares on the legs (Side A and Side B) equals the area of the square on the hypotenuse (Side C). This formula is attributed the Greek mathematician Pythagoras, who lived from 570 BC to 495 BC. The Pythagorean Theory has been interesting to non-mathematicians as a symbol of mystique and intellectual power — there are popular references to this theory in literature, plays, musicals, songs, stamps, and even cartoons!

25 — C. 10 yards

The circumference (C) of a circle of radius R is the following:

$$C = 2\pi R$$

The radius of the circle is expressed as:

$$R = C/2\pi$$

The question asks for an approximate answer; the "rounded off" value of π ("pi") is 3.14. If the circumference is 190 feet, you can now substitute it into the equation:

$$R = 190/(2 * \pi)$$
$$R = 190/(2 * 3.14)$$
$$R = 30.25 \text{ feet}$$

Since 1 yard equals 3 feet, 30.25 feet ÷ 3 = 10.1 or approximately 10 yards.

26 — C. 4:1 or 400%

First, since the area of a circle is determined using the radius (R), remember that the radius of Circle A is 50 feet; i.e. half of the circle's diameter.

$$A = \pi R^2$$

$$A_{Circle\ A} = \pi * 50^2$$

$A_{Circle\ A}$ = 3.14 * 2,500
$A_{Circle\ A}$ = 7,850 miles^2

$A_{Circle\ B}$ = π * 25^2
$A_{Circle\ B}$ = 3.14 * 625
$A_{Circle\ B}$ = 1,962.5 miles^2

*T*o determine the relationship of the two circle's areas, divide the two values just found:

Ratio = $A_{Circle\ A}$ ÷ $A_{Circle\ B}$
Ratio = 7,850 ÷ 1,962.5
Ratio = 4:1 or 400% larger

Therefore, Circle A is four times bigger than Circle B, even though it's radius is only twice as big! The reason is that when you are calculating the area of a circle, you are taking the radius value to the second power; i.e. multiplying it by itself.

27 — A. 2x² + 5x - 12

Multiplying the two binomials together with FOIL means that the first term is the product of x and 2x, or 2x². Therefore, you can eliminate answers B and D.

However, the last term is the product of 4 and -3, which equals -12, which means that answer C is an incorrect answer. Since the middle term is the sum of 8x and -3x, which is 5x, answer A is the only correct answer. If you choose to use the box method to solve these products, you will see the same results and the same factors.

28 — A. 2x² + 6x - 8

Multiplying the two binomials together with FOIL means that the first term is the product of x and 2x or 2x². Therefore, eliminate answers B and D.

However the last term is the product of 4 and -2 which means that answer C is an incorrect answer. Since the middle term is the sum of 8x and -2x, which is 6x, answer A is the only correct answer. If you choose to use the box method to solve these products you will see the same results and the same factors.

29 — B. 3x² - 4x - 15

The words in the problem tell you that the new expression for the length is 3x+5 and the new width is represented by the expression x-3. The area is represented by the product of (3x+5) (x-3). Multiplying the two binomials together with FOIL means that the first term is the product of x and 3x, or 3x². All of the multiple choices have the correct first term. However, the last term is the product of 5 and -3, or -15, which means that answer C is an incorrect answer.

Since the middle term is the difference between 5x and -9x, which is -4x, answer B is the only correct answer. If you choose to use the box method to solve these products, you will see the same results and the same factors.

30 — C. 14x² +13x + 3

The words in the problem tell you that the new expression for the base is 4x+2 and the new height is represented by the expression 7x+3. The area is represented by the product of 1/2(4x+2)(7x+3). Multiplying the two binomials together with FOIL means that the first term is the product of 4x and 7x and 1/2, or 14x². All of the multiple choices have the correct first term.

However, the last term is the product of 2 and 3 and 1/2, or 3, which means that answer A is an incorrect answer.

The middle term is 1/2 the sum of 14x and 12x, which is 26/2 x, or 13x. Therefore, answer C is the only correct answer. If you choose to use the box method to solve these products, you will see the same results and the same factors.

31 — B. x > 16/7

The inequality can be solved by finding the equality:

14x - 8 = 24

Add 8 to both sides: 14x = 32

Divide both sides by 14: x = 32 / 14, or 16 / 7

To check for the correct direction of the inequality, test with x = 0. The inequality means that: -8 > 24, which is not true. Since 0 does not satisfy the inequality, the correct values of x must be greater than 16/7, since 0 is less than 16/7.

32 — C. x < 33/5

The inequality can be solved by finding the equality:

5x + 16 = 49

Subtract 16 from both sides: 5x = 33
Divide both sides by 5: x = 33 / 5

To check for the correct direction of the inequality, test with x = 0. The inequality means that: 16 < 49, which is true. Since 0 satisfies the inequality, the correct values of x must be less than 33/5, since 0 is less than 33/5.

FINAL THOUGHTS

Congratulations!

If you're reading this, that means you have successfully completed your first experience with the Spire Study System, a fresh new approach to studying. You've proven that you're one of the free thinkers of the world, willing to try new things and challenge conventional wisdom.

We sincerely hope you enjoyed the Spire Study System for the ACCUPLACER (...well, as much as anyone can enjoy studying — you know what we mean).

If we succeeded and you're impressed with the Spire Study System, or if you have suggestions about how we can improve, we'd love to hear from you! Our inbox is always open: contact@spirestudysystem.com.

Better yet, tell your friends about us. And be sure to look for our upcoming books. We can't wait to bring the Spire Study System to more students!

Best Wishes,

Your study partners at Spire